CHOSEN AND SENT

CHOSEN AND SENT

Calling the Church to Mission

A. THEODORE EASTMAN

WILLIAM B. EERDMANS PUBLISHING COMPANY
GRAND RAPIDS, MICHIGAN

To
Richard Coombs,
Kenneth Heim
and
Max Warren,
colleagues, mentors, friends,
who, having been chosen
and sent themselves,
have shown me
and many others
ways to respond.

EDITORIAL FOREWORD

The popular slogans "one-world mission" and "mission in six continents" are frequently interpreted to mean witness and service by the disciple and the local church just where they happen to exist. Although they put a new emphasis on "world," they tend to limit the meaning of that "world" to the immediate neighborhood or at most to the nation by stressing the inescapable call to local proclamation and to an encounter with American (or Western) technological, urban society. The broader and equally imperative ministry and service to the rest of the world is forgotten. Today on the university campus "the third world," for example, no longer means the developing new nations, but the Blacks and Puerto Ricans of the city slums and very occasionally the American Indians. But Mr. Eastman has the church in the entire world—here and everywhere—in view as he discusses "the call," "the response," and "the response in action." Here, in the perspective of the Bible and of church history, is a clear and convincing statement of the meaning of God's calling and sending his church into the totality of human society in the final third of the twentieth century.

This volume is one of Eerdmans' CHRISTIAN WORLD MISSION BOOKS and takes its place in the series "Ministries in Mission."

R. Pierce Beaver
Editor

CONTENTS

ACKNOWLEDGMENTS

Grateful acknowledgment is given to the following publishers and authors for permission to reprint copyrighted material from the titles listed below:

The Center Magazine, a publication of the Center for the Study of Democratic Institutions, Santa Barbara, California—Peter Ustinov, "I Propose a New Tradition," January, 1969.

Christian Comment, Manchester, England—Basil Higginson, "The Samaritans," October, 1968.

The Church Review, Cambridge, Massachusetts—Myron B. Bloy, Jr., "Alienated Youth, Their Counter Culture, and the Chaplain," November, 1968.

The Ecumenist, New York—Gregory Baum, "A Roman Catholic Reaction," January-February, 1968.

Wm. B. Eerdmans Publishing Co., Grand Rapids, Michigan—Michael P. Hamilton (ed.), *The Vietnam War: Christian Perspectives.* Used by permission.

Herder and Herder, New York—Roger Garaudy, *From Anathema to Dialogue.*

Holt, Rinehart and Winston, New York—Stephen C. Rose, *The Grass Roots Church.*

The Macmillan Co., New York—Harvey Cox, *The Secular City.*

The National Council of Churches of Christ in the U.S.A., New York—Colin F. Williams, *What in the World?* Copyright © 1964 by Colin F. Williams. Used with permission.

The New York *Times*—Edward B. Fiske, "Catholic Underground Churches Grow," April 22, 1968. © 1968 by the New York Times Company. Reprinted by permission.

Penguin Books, Ltd., Harmondsworth—C. L. Rieu (tr.), *The Acts of the Apostles by St. Luke.*

SCM Press, Ltd., London—J. G. Davies, *Dialogue with the World.*

Charles Scribner's Sons, New York—Arend Th. van Leeuwen, *Christianity and World History*; H. J. Schultz, *Conversion to the World.*

The author also wishes to express his deep gratitude to those who have been instrumental in the preparation of this book: to the people of St. Barnabas Church, Irvington, N. Y., and their former rector, the Rev. David R. Matlack, and the people of St. Peter's Church, Charlotte, N. C., and their rector, the Rev. Huntington Williams, Jr., for preaching invitations which first prompted me to develop the themes reflected in the initial five chapters; to the officers and managers of the Overseas Mission Society, who granted me a sabbatical leave during which the writing began; to the Renewal Commission of the Episcopal Church and its chairman, the Rt. Rev. Anson P. Stokes, Jr., who permitted me time to complete and revise the manuscript; to John and Ingrid Plant, whose vacant Vienna apartment provided a much-needed quiet place to read, think and write; to Ellen N. Sherk, who skillfully typed and retyped seemingly endless drafts; and to Prof. R. Pierce Beaver, a most patient and charitable editor.

A. Theodore Eastman

I

INTRODUCTION

The natural erosions of time and the ordinary stresses of history require Christians to make repeated, thorough inspections of the vehicle which has carried their company through a succession of centuries. When the climate is adverse and the going difficult, as it is today, it is especially necessary to test the world-worthiness of the church. By "world-worthiness" I mean the ability of the church to facilitate the arrival of Christians at their appointed destination: true encounter, effective engagement with men and societies.

Platoons of contemporary analysts are carefully at work examining the church. They are detecting numerous defects. Some inspectors advise scrapping the old familiar mechanism entirely, replacing it with a completely new model of as yet undetermined specifications. Other probers suggest, in varying degrees, that adaptation will suffice.

Whether one agrees with the need for fresh designs or subscribes to the prescription of pragmatic adjustments, the current course of evaluations has revealed two basic weaknesses, which require considerable and immediate attention. First, it is now evident that the fundamental driving force of this conveyance called the church is not sufficient to propel its passengers purposefully through these restless, questing times. That is to say, the traditional basis of the Christian mission no longer motivates many men. Second, the body of the vehicle is far too brittle and cumbersome to bear the strains placed upon it by the fast-moving, quickly shifting traffic of the modern world. That is to say, the traditional structures of the church, as they have been constructed, equipped, and adapted for missions past, are now so rigidly fixed that the central task has begun to be shaped by the design rather than served by it.

The purpose of this book is to examine these two particular defects in the life and mission of the modern church—inadequate motivation and insufficient flexibility—in such a way as to make a small contribution to the many studies needed to correct them.

* * *

The biblical material out of which the church's missionary consciousness, comprehension, and compliance have commonly been drawn is neatly distilled in the words of the Great Commission, found at the end of Matthew's Gospel (28:19-20), with variations in the other Synoptic Gospels (Mark 16:15-16; Luke 24:47-48) and in Acts (1:8). This simple scriptural command—to go and make disciples of all nations—has much to commend it as a continuing source of fuel for the Christian mission. It is linked to Jesus himself. It is a clear and concise set of orders. The history of its propelling power, particularly through the past several centuries, gives it momentum and mystique.

At the same time, however, there are problems hidden in this depictive distillation. Despite its attribution to Jesus, modern biblical scholarship disputes the authenticity of the Great Commission. The Markan version is especially in doubt. A second problem is its familiarity. While frequent use doesn't necessarily lead to obsolescence, it can dull the keenness of even the most serviceable of instruments. In addition there is what may be called "the paradox of mere obedience." Command-obey relationships have always been difficult for men. And it is certain that emancipated, independent citizens of the twentieth century seek a more compelling, reasoned (or perhaps emotional) motivation for their mission than someone's say-so, whether "someone" be capitalized or not. And if these problems aren't sufficient to sap the strength from the Great Commission, the fourth liability is. To balance the missionary imperative on so narrow an injunction as this, which is precisely where it is poised for most ordinary Christians, is to invite total collapse when tremors of doubt or distress begin.

Following an age of surging missionary zeal, contemporary Christians are experiencing a massive breakdown of confidence in the fullness of their mission. Because this collapse is taking place gradually and piecemeal, it is not dramatically apparent to many. But it is happening nonetheless. It occurs wherever one part of the church is consumed with concern for a local need or opportunity to the exclusion of other, more distant responsibilities. It occurs whenever evangelism is distorted to mean rechurching lapsed or migrant Christians on the one hand or gathering converts, as an ardent hobbyist collects coins or stamps, on the other hand.

The downfall of the Great Commission as the symbol of an oversimplified understanding of mission is driving contemporary theologians to search the Bible afresh for clues to the central calling of the church. In his book *Dialogue with the World,* J. G. Davies sums up the effort to transform all Christian theology into a theology of mission. Describing God as "a centrifugal being," he says,

> The living God of the bible is revealed to us as essentially a sending God. Only a cursory glance through the books of the Old Testament serves to endorse this view. God is one who sends help (Ps. 20.2); he sends pestilence (Ezek. 14.19); he sends fear (Ex. 23.27); he sends a sword (Jer. 9.16); he sends redemption (Ps. 111.9). God sends his angels (Ex. 23.20); he sends individuals such as Moses (Ex. 3.10) or Gideon (Judg. 6.14); God sends the prophets (Jer. 7.25), and such men as Isaiah, Jeremiah and Ezekiel are convinced that they have been sent (Isa. 6.8; Jer. 1.7; Ezek. 2.3). The picture that emerges from the New Testament is essentially the same. God sends his Son (John 17.18); he sends the Holy Spirit (John 14.26).

> So mission is not simply obedience to a divine command, to an injunction of the exalted Christ, the authenticity of which may be questioned; mission is the taking up of man actively into God's design.[1]

It is God's nature to send. But before he does so, he must choose whom he will send. He *calls* and commissions. He *selects* and sends. He *decides upon* and dispatches. God called to Moses out of the burning bush (Exod. 3:4) and sent him to lead his captive people out of Egypt. The angel of the Lord called Gideon away from threshing in his wine press (Judg. 6:11-12) and sent him to defeat the Midianites. God called the vision-dazzled Ezekiel to his feet by the River Chebar (Ezek. 2:1) and sent him to goad the recalcitrant Israelites. God called to Isaiah in the temple and asked him whom he should send to be a prophet for his people (Isa. 6:8), prompting the young man to respond, "Here I am! Send me." Through his son, Jesus, God called Simon and Andrew (Mark 1:16) and sent them to be fishers of men. On a desert road the Lord called to the prostrate Saul (Acts 9:3-6), sending him on to Damascus and the rest of the Roman world as an apostle to the Gentiles.

These great biblical figures are, of course, only representative of millions of men who have been called by God, who have responded to him, who have been sent on many errands across the span of history. All but a few of their names have been lost or forgotten. And all but a small percentage of them have executed their callings outside of the narrow realm of religion. For God sends men to fulfill his will within their natural communities, through the ordinary structures of the world, and those he sends are not always the ones who believe in him. To analyze the process of choosing and sending, therefore, is not a simple matter. Some persons, like those spectacular heroes of the Bible, believe they have received a direct, objective summons from God. Others do not. Some find a source of power and perspective for their calling within the community of faith. Others do not. Yet all exist under the purview of God's providence.

Although men may respond to God anywhere and everywhere, consciously or unconsciously, alone or in groups, this book is primarily concerned with those who attend and answer within that segment of society called the church. The church requires special attention, not because it has greater relevance than other social structures, but because it has a singular self-consciousness about the order of creation and the activity of God. That intrinsic awareness, and its function within the human setting, needs to be better understood today, especially in relation to the equally unique missions of other men and communities. So, while parallel areas of recognized or unrecognized response cannot be ignored, they will be considered in this study only when they bear on our primary subject, the church.

If the transaction of calling and sending is God's way of taking man actively into his design, to employ Professor Davies' image, what is the specific nature of the Christian response, both personally and corporately? Where do alert Christians or responsive churches get their bearings? What are their relationships to the world of which they are parts? How do they proceed with their tasks? What guarantees their pertinence and effectiveness?

As I noted earlier in connection with the Matthean Commission, any narrow-gauge passage of Scripture is too cramped an area in which to discover adequate reference points for mission today. Only the entire range of the Bible provides the kind of scope modern man requires. Yet it is impossible to examine the entire Bible within the confines of a book so small as this one. As an exercise in looking more broadly for clues to the nature of the Christian calling, we need to focus on a specific portion of the Bible, one which is limited in size but sufficiently roomy for exploration. The tenth chapter of Matthew, for instance, provides plenty of space in which to roam and probe; the complete Book of Acts even more. And the post-resurrection appearances in all four Gospels contain an ample array of suggestive words and images.

For our purposes, however, there are five compelling chapters in the Fourth Gospel, which combine continuity with the kind of elbow room we need. They are John 13-17, a segment often described as "the farewell discourses." In the fourth evangelist's account these five chapters directly precede the final conflict leading to the Lord's death. They present what is probably the best sustained example in the New Testament of Jesus' reasoned yet impassioned counsel with his closest followers. If we believe anything about his wisdom and forethought, they—or something like them—must be seen to be the culmination of a period of well-considered preparation designed by Jesus to equip the disciples for the continuation of his mission.

That such a set of contiguous, culminating discourses should appear in the Fourth Gospel rather than in the other three is neither accidental nor surprising, given the contrasting circumstances in which the various accounts were written. Comparison indicates why these discourses may contain or prompt insights which will help latter day Christians understand their mission with greater clarity. The Synoptic Gospels (Matthew, Mark, Luke) are journalistic in approach, largely concerned with concrete actions and proper chronology. John's Gospel, by contrast, is reflective and interpretive. The Synoptics represent an earlier rendering of the oral tradition. John's account was written later, assimilating the main facts and broad chronology of the previous records, and putting them into perspective. The first three Gospels are Palestinian in orientation, revealing the coloration of early Christianity in its natural semitic habitat. The Fourth Gospel, being later, was written as the church began to confront the Gentile world, reflecting both the external conflict with different sets of religio-cultural presuppositions and standards and the internal tensions of trying to adapt to them in order to make contact and be understood. In this sense the context out of which the Gospel of John was produced is strangely parallel to the situation in which the twentieth-century church finds itself.[2] Discourses in the Synoptic Gospels are primarily addressed either to local religious leaders in Galilee, as in the synagogue in Nazareth, or the multitudes, as in the Sermon on the Mount. Discourses in John are mainly directed to the religious leaders in Jerusalem or, more significantly, to the inner group of disciples.

As John recounts them, the farewell discourses quite clearly begin in the well-known upper room, probably during or at the end of Jesus' last supper with his inner circle. Commentators disagree about whether they took place there in their entirety—or whether they even occurred in sequence at all. There are some indications that Jesus and the group left the room (14:31). At least one of the images Jesus used (the vine, in chapter 15) suggests that they may have walked to the temple as they continued their conversations. Nevertheless, the upper room is a locale consistent with the tone of the discourses; the crucial content of these talks would seem to have required quiet and concentration.

Although Matthew and Mark describe in detail the events which led up to the Last Supper, they are virtually silent about what actually transpired around the table. Luke fills in some of the gaps. But it is John who rounds out the scene, assuming that the reader is familiar with the earlier Synoptic accounts. From the fourth evangelist's standpoint it seems clear that Jesus knew a great watershed moment was approaching. His own mission was about to be ended abruptly, which meant that it would have to be assumed and continued in a new way by his disciples. He wanted to explain to them, quietly and rationally, what was about to happen to him, why it was necessary, and what the disciples' response should be. He wished to make all this clear before the agony and confusion of the last moments arrived. His own words reveal the aim of these final discourses: Referring to his certain betrayal he said, "I tell you this now, before the event, that when it happens you may believe that I am what I am" (13:19 NEB). After predicting the persecution his

followers would face he said, "I have told you all this so that when
the time comes for it to happen you may remember my warning. I
did not tell you this at first, because I was with you; but now I am
going away to him who sent me" (16:4-5 NEB).

The thoughts that Jesus shared with his disciples, as compiled and
arranged by the fourth evangelist, come through in a somewhat
disjoined, repetitive, and overlapping fashion. Rather than writing
this record off as an incompetent job of reporting and editing, we
can see it as a skillful setting of a scene of rambling, free-flowing
conversation in a room full of well-acquainted people. Anyone who
has played back tape recordings of conversations held under similar
circumstances will understand the mood of that moment.

In any case, out of this loose conglomeration of dramatic actions,
long monologues, quick repartee, and brief by-plays, four fundamental themes may be isolated. Jesus undoubtedly intended to
communicate these basic ideas to the twelve and to the others who
were present in that room and through them to the incipient church.
They continue to bear directly on the central task of the church
today. They pertain to the *basis* of the Christian mission, the *context*
and *manner* of that mission and the *power* required to fulfill it.

* * *

Before turning to an extended consideration of these major
motifs, a comment must be made about the importance of the last
segment of the farewell discourses: Chapter 17, the powerful
high-priestly prayer. While this prayer stands magnificently by itself,
it is very much an integral part of the discourses, not because it
represents another theme, but because it provides a kind of accent
mark over each of the others. That accent mark, which clarifies and
enhances the four central topics of the discourses, is the note of
unity.

Since primitive times a priest of religion has been one set apart to
stand between the human and divine elements of reality. Through his
sacral actions he seeks to bridge the gap separating man from his
god. In a sense his function is to bring the two together in his own
person. With its own unique variation, that priestly role is
particularly evident in the great prayer of John 17. In it Jesus offers
himself, as both priest and victim, to be an atoning sacrifice for the
world—to restore the broken relationship between God's will and
man's desire, to make them *at one* again. But he goes farther. He
enlarges his own consecration significantly by incorporating into this

unifying process both his immediate disciples and the church throughout the ages to come. References to his overriding concern for unity are shot through the entire prayer (vv. 1, 8, 10, 11, 21-23, 26).

Unity may be the wrong word to use, because it connotes the absence of diversity. Perhaps *wholeness* is a better term to express the concept suggested by John 17. Rooted in the Middle English word for health, *wholeness* describes the condition which obtains when all of the diverse parts of an organism are sound and working well together. Moreover *wholeness* may be said to rejoice in diversity, as long as coordination and mutual respect exist.

Wholeness is the touchstone of God's activity and, therefore, of the Christian mission. Wherever barriers which divide men and imprison them in their own ignorance and prejudice are broken down, wherever breakthroughs in knowledge demolish fragmentary views of the universe, wherever mutual understanding is achieved in the world, wherever reconciliation is operative, there God's will to wholeness has struck a responsive chord in mankind. Whenever churches or individual Christians, who are meant to be unusually sensitive to the mind of God, act as agents of wholeness they are faithfully fulfilling their commission. For the goal of divine activity, which encompasses every area of life and every field of human endeavor, is to set men free and make them whole by unifying all creation again under the sovereign reign of God. The consequent aim of the church, as the company of disciples of the one God, is to assist that process, not just by reuniting itself, though that is useful, but by seeking to provide the cement which binds together human relationships, even as the apostles of discord disseminate a solvent which disintegrates them. That aim is meant to be pursued to the outer limits of time, space, and knowledge with all of the wisdom, all of the resources, and all of the openness to the power of God's spirit that a human community can muster. By seeking to foster wholeness in every segment of life they touch, including their own internal life, Christians testify that they are at one with God's will, even as Jesus was of one mind with the Father. When that becomes evident to the world, then the world may begin to understand what the harmonizing, unifying love of God is all about.

The need for wholeness has been a part of human history since the beginning, but seldom has it been felt with such keen urgency as today. Gregory Baum, the theologian and ecumenist, believes that it is the primary quest of modern man. In a recent address, he said:

> Some questions asked by the ancients, and some asked in the 16th century, are no longer questions which we ask with great urgency. It seems to me that the questions we ask today mainly deal with friendship and reconciliation across conflict. We experience ourselves as a divided world, a world threatened by conflicts: man against man, race against race, party against party. We discover the isolation produced by sin. We know the painful isolation of people in our big cities and the problem of their personal identity. We are convinced, by the Gospel, that the way of fellowship and reconciliation is the only way of finding oneself. For this reason, I think, we experience God today as unifier and reconciler, as initiating us into friendship and consequently self-appropriation. What are our great spiritual experiences today? They are usually experiences of groups, of fellowship, of movements. I believe therefore that the ecumenical movement, the coming together of Christians from different traditions, with different historical experiences, yet reaching beyond this to experience the Gospel together— this is in itself an experience of God as he manifests himself to us today. I believe that the reconciliation of people is today an answer to our crisis of faith.[3]

If that is an accurate description of the current condition to which the Gospel speaks, then it is also the central challenge to the contemporary church. It is into that setting that Christians are called by God to go with conviction and flexibility. Now let us consider the characteristics of that conviction and the forms which that flexibility may take.

PART ONE

THE CALL

II

THE NATURE OF THE MISSION

"I am the real vine, and my Father is the gardener. Every barren branch of mine he cuts away; and every fruiting branch he cleans, to make it more fruitful still. You have already been cleansed by the word that I spoke to you. Dwell in me, as I in you. No branch can bear fruit by itself, but only if it remains united with the vine; no more can you bear fruit, unless you remain united with me.

"I am the vine and you the branches. He who dwells in me, as I dwell in him, bears much fruit; for apart from me you can do nothing. He who does not dwell in me is thrown away like a withered branch. The withered branches are heaped together, thrown on the fire, and burnt.

"If you dwell in me, and my words dwell in you, ask what you will, and you shall have it. This is my Father's glory, that you may bear fruit in plenty and so be my disciples. As the Father has loved me, so I have loved you. Dwell in my love. If you heed my commands, you will dwell in my love, as I have heeded my Father's commands and dwell in his love.

"I have spoken thus to you, so that my joy may be in you, and your joy complete. This is my commandment: love one another, as I have loved you. There is no greater love than this,

that a man should lay down his life for his friends. You are my friends, if you do what I command you. I call you servants no longer; a servant does not know what his master is about. I have called you friends, because I have disclosed to you everything that I heard from my Father. You did not choose me: I chose you. I appointed you to go on and bear fruit, fruit that shall last; so that the Father may give you all that you ask in my name. This is my commandment to you: love one another."

John 15:1-17(NEB)

According to many scholars, there was fixed over the gate of the temple in Jerusalem during Jesus' lifetime a great, ornate sculpture of a vine, done in relief, probably fashioned of metal and plated with gold. It was seen frequently by every devout Jew in the city. So striking and prominent was this image that even the occasional worshipper or the most casual visitor would have been aware of it. To those who knew their Scriptures the significance of the sculpture was obvious, for in the Old Testament, Israel is often identified with the grapevine. There are references to this effect in Ezekiel (15:1-8), Psalms (80:8-16), Isaiah (5:1-5), and elsewhere. Almost without exception, however, each comparison of Israel with the vine ends on a note of corruption, failure, or destruction.

While not all of the disciples were zealous practitioners of Judaism, the image of the vine and its connection with Israel was doubtless imprinted clearly on the mind of each. So when Jesus reached into the Scriptures and grasped this figure of speech during his final instructions in the upper room, they would have been right with him, though they were probably surprised by his new interpretation. "*I* am the ... vine," he said, indicating that he himself was the personification of the metaphor and the fulfiller of its meaning in a way that Israel could never be. He turned the figure away from God's chosen but reluctant people, applied it to himself, as the new and faithful instrument of divine initiative, and then drew those who were closest to him into the very heart of the figure too. In doing this he made three things clear.

First, in contrast to a mere imitation—like the rigid, lifeless, pretentious vine that symbolized Israel over the entrance to the temple—a living cellulose and chlorophyll vine is dependent upon the grower. As the grapevine is tended by the farmer, who cultivates, waters, and fertilizes the ground, ties and prunes the branches, and gathers the fruit, so he is thoroughly cared for by his Father, whom he calls "the gardener."

Complete submission to the strict guidance and patient nurture of the vinedresser, then, is a sign of the authentic vine. In this Jesus, unlike Israel, has been faithful.

Referring to van Peursen's study of the Old Testament use of the Hebrew noun *emeth* ("truth"), Harvey Cox points out that the word designates

> something that can be counted on, something that is found to be dependable. It is used to refer to a vine which bears fruit, as expected, in the fall. God is spoken of as true because He does what He says He will do. He delivers the slaves from captivity and is thus true to His people. Performance is the yardstick of truth.[1]

Jesus, in this sense, is the *true* vine because he is dependable. He produces as he says he will.

There is not only a qualitative aspect to the figure of the vine but a quantitative one as well. Jesus did not say, "I am the root of the vine," or "I am the stem of the vine." Rather he said, "I am the . . . *vine.*" He is the entire plant: root, stem, branches, tendrils, leaves, grapes. *He* is the whole vine. *He* is the new Israel. In *him* the order of things is radically changed. The mission is essentially *his.*

How this conflicts with our contemporary assumptions and images! Often we act as if the Father were chairman of the board of the enterprise, Jesus the president, and the Holy Spirit the executive vice president. This triumvirate at the top is known to wield great power behind the scenes, but is seldom seen around the premises by those of us who do the actual work. Jesus rebukes us, even in our more sophisticated fantasies, with the simple reminder that he is the works, the complete business—or, in the appropriate rural idiom of his day, the entire vine.

With this in mind Christians only dare use such terms as "the Christian mission" or "the mission of the church" with the greatest sensitivity, with the lightest possible touch. Certain labels are inescapable, for all men are captives of their own particular vocabularies. But Christians always need to be absolutely clear, as J. G. Davies reminds us, that the church does not plan *its* mission and then proceed with the divine assistance; the Spirit takes the initiative; he goes on ahead. He says: "Set apart for me Barnabas and Saul for the work to which I have called them". ... Mission *is* a divine activity. God is both the source of the missionary enterprise and the one who retains it in his own hands, nor does he surrender it to any human authority.[2]

Jesus, in whom God's activity had been concentrated in a unique way, employed a metaphor to challenge man's impertinence. But he also used it to reveal man's proper participation in the mission of God. If the analogy of the vine suggests the relationship of the Son to the Father, it also indicates the connection of the disciples to the Son, which leads to the second point hidden in the image. As the vine cannot exist without the gardener, so the branches cannot live apart from the vine. Nor, alternatively, can the vine bear fruit without the branches. This is a relationship of planned interdependence, which is the way God has chosen to continue the creation and renewal of his world. The link between the farmer and the fruit is the vine. The link between God and his agents of renewal is the Son of Man, Jesus of Nazareth.

A thorough search of the creation story of Genesis, as Harvey Cox reminds us, shows that man was meant to share a cooperative role with God from the beginning. He points out that biblical scholars have long been charmed by Greek philosophy, which has led them to overlook or minimize the fact that

creation is *not* completed by God in the Bible until after man is formed and begins to work as God's partner in ordering the chaos. This means, in effect, that creation is *never* really "complete." The Genesis stories depict something that man and God are always doing. Part of the error of Christian philosophy has arisen from a rather mechanical insistence on a *creatio ex nihilo*. Without denying that God does bring the world into being out of nothing, we must go on to see, with Gerhard von Rad, that this is not the real point. The concern of the Genesis narrative "moves not so much between the poles of nothingness and creation as between the poles of chaos and cosmos." God orders the chaos by giving it names ("God called the light Day, and the darkness he called Night," v.3). Man participates along with God by naming the living creatures (2:20) and the woman (3:20). Together God and man devise the emblems and meanings by which anarchic confusion becomes a world. When we read the record this way, the tyrant God of both atheism and theism disappears, and the partnership of God and man comes into focus.[3]

Partnership, the word Cox uses to describe the cooperation of God and man, is graphic. But its contractual overtones must not be permitted to distort the connotation of profound interdependence, for the relationship it describes is an intensely dynamic one.

Jesus expressed the nature of the divine-human interdependence, which he perceived deeply within his own being, by using the concept of mutual indwelling. "Dwell in me, as I in you," he said, in a clearly imperative tone. He knew that if there is to be a fruitful partnership, then mutual indwelling is essential. It is the source of relevance and power. It is the aim of all sound Christian devotion and discipline. Prayer and liturgical worship are meant to provide Christians with a regularly renewed sense of responsible interdependence with God, not necessarily in the mode of mysticism (which seems to be a closed option for most pragmatic, contemporary men), but in a conscious and rational (though perhaps occasionally exciting and evocative) way. The central intent of the Holy Communion or Eucharist, regarded by most Christians as the capstone of worship, is simply "that he may dwell in us, and we in him."[4] That is an old fashioned—but biblical—way of declaring that the contract in this partnership stands in need of periodic renewal and that powers need to be exchanged afresh.

It is at this point that the accent mark of unity or wholeness comes into play. To make sense of life we need to see ourselves as part of a larger whole. To accomplish anything of lasting value we need a purpose and a strength greater than our own. That unity of perspective, purpose, and power, Christians believe, proceeds from God, as we have come to understand him through the life and ministry of Jesus. Thus no Christian disciple in any age can claim originality, for his part is to let God's creativity find expression through his own unique but derivative intelligence. A recognition of this is undoubtedly what led Paul, that irrepressible but genuinely humble theologian and missionary, to compose as his motto, "not I, but Christ in me."[5] When the unity of perspective, purpose, and power required for the dynamic interdependence of God's joint venture with man is recognized and maintained, the mission functions smoothly. But when any part of the church allows itself to be cut off from the mind of Christ, the result is a sick soul, a paralyzed parish, or a dead denomination—in effect, a moribund mission.

The third point which Jesus made plain through the figure of the vine is that the worth of the disciples will be measured by their productivity. When he said, "This is my father's glory, that you may bear fruit in plenty and so be my disciples," it was not instantly apparent what kind of fruit he expected of the disciples. But then he went on to explain that the bearing of fruit is based on the commandment of love, which means to empty one's self, to sacrifice one's private needs for the sake of others. As a portent of what was about to engulf him personally, Jesus pointed to the extreme example of love in action: "There is no greater love than this, that a man should lay down his life for his friends" (v. 13).

Bearing fruit, then, is an exercise in extroversion. Devotional ardor—if it is introverted, if it is engaged in merely to sustain the self—is not compatible with true discipleship. Ascetic discipline—if it is isolated from the needs of the world—is not congruous with a productive mission. God is not praised by paying him personal and pious attention. He is truly glorified—and men receive valid credentials of discipleship—when those who have been chosen are found in the process of losing themselves in behalf of the world.

It is possible, of course, to be called into life by God and to respond with a certain amount of growth, but not to bear fruit. Blocked somehow from the source of the vine's vitality, certain branches are stunted, and they wither and die. When the winds of stress blow, many of the lifeless limbs cannot prevail and fall to the earth. Those that remain are lopped off by the vinedresser. Having lost all meaning by becoming functionless, the dead branches are gathered together, heaped on the fire and burned. Emptiness ends in destruction.

Judas Iscariot is probably the classic example of the barren branch, the non-responsive disciple. The church has always had within its ranks a number of his successors. In order to correct the situation, Jesus implied, a periodic cleansing of the church is necessary, painful though it may be. Sensitive observers can see this withering, pruning, burning process taking place in churches across the world today. In Russia, in parts of Europe, in China, in Cuba, in certain post-colonial sectors of Africa and Asia where the prestige of the church is in eclipse due to ideological hostility, political pressure, or lack of respect, fringe members have dropped away while large numbers of new members have failed to develop.

In the United States (and perhaps elsewhere) the sloughing-off process begins in several ways. On the one hand there are those churchmen who consider Christianity to be little more than personal religion and only vaguely and indirectly connected with the central human issues of the day. They find themselves more and more isolated from the quality of faith which surges into every aspect of life. Gradually they fall away into pious irrelevance. On the other hand there are those church members who are so easily swayed by every wind of change that they are constantly accommodating to the standards of society in general. Eventually, like the tumbleweed, they find themselves uprooted from the objective judgment of the faith. In either case the prophetic force of the gospel is perilously stifled, stunted, shriveled.

In pondering the phenomenon of barrenness, it must be remembered that the branches are not meant to assess each other's worthiness. Some unproductive members are stripped away in the gales of adversity. Some drop off the vine from sheer dead weight. Some are judiciously pruned at the proper time—by the gardener. Ultimately it is only God himself who judges which limbs are fruitful and which are not.

Good husbandry demands that barren boughs be cut away; it also requires that fruitful branches be trimmed in order to be more productive still. Various efforts which may seem only partly successful or even totally unfulfilled may not be failures at all. Fresh starts or new growth may stem from such experiences. Considered in this light, trial and difficulty can be seen to be beneficial, perhaps even necessary, to the health of the branch and the well-being of the entire vine. Without making the metaphor an apology for divine manipulation, it may be argued that indifference, even persecution, if kept in perspective, is instructive and ultimately strengthening for Christians and the church.

Implicit in Jesus' understanding of himself as the real vine was the consistent expectation of his own obliteration. For even as the branches of the vine are pruned, so also is the whole vine cut back at the end of a season. Thus this great and powerful image ends by facing us toward a hillock outside the walls of Jerusalem where the one, authentic, representative vine allowed himself to be hewn down level with the ground. The axe of human willfulness did its worst. The withered, lifeless vine hung limp upon the trellis. Yet that was not the end. A dying was needed so that in due time new life could spring forth through the vine and into all the branches. The dependability of Jesus, the true vine, made his passion and death an inevitable result of his mission. To the degree that the branches perform with like consistency, mission will lead through passion for them as well.

The metaphor of the vine, then, offers the Christian clues to the nature of his calling. The mission in which all men are invited to participate is none other than God's continuing action of making his creation whole, that is, complete and integrated under his just and supreme rule of love. The pattern of that ongoing mission has become concrete and clear in the life and ministry of Jesus of Nazareth, the fully responsive and dependable person, who elicits in other men the will to become partners with God in creating worldly wholeness. Those who consciously respond to Jesus, and as a consequence call themselves Christians, find they can be effective co-creators only as they are congruent with his mind and united in his spirit. But such constancy carries with it great danger in face of the forces of divisiveness and rebellion in this world, which is the context of the mission.

III

THE CONTEXT OF THE MISSION

"If the world hated you, it hated me first, as you know well. If you belonged to the world, the world would love its own; but because you do not belong to the world, because I have chosen you out of the world, for that reason the world hates you. Remember what I said: 'A servant is not greater than his master.' As they persecuted me, they will persecute you; they will follow your teaching as little as they have followed mine. It is on my account that they will treat you thus, because they do not know the One who sent me.

"If I had not come and spoken to them, they would not be guilty of sin; but now they have no excuse for their sin: he who hates me, hates my Father. If I had not worked among them and accomplished what no other man has done, they would not be guilty of sin; but now they have both seen and hated both me and my Father. However, this text in their Law had to come true: 'They hated me without reason.'

"But when your Advocate has come, whom I will send you from the Father—the Spirit of truth that issues from the Father—he will bear witness to me. And you also are my witnesses, because you have been with me from the first.

"I have told you all this to guard you against the breakdown

*of your faith. They will ban you from the synagogue; indeed,
the time is coming when anyone who kills you will suppose
that he is performing a religious duty. They will do these
things because they do not know either the Father or me."*
                                                    John 15:18-16:3(NEB)

Jesus spoke with sobering clarity and power about the kind of
reception the disciples would get as they attempted to continue his
mission in the world. He warned them that they could expect
nothing less than rejection, hatred, persecution, and death, generated
not only by the legions of the world (15:18-19) but by the forces of
organized religion as well (16:1-2). To grasp the full range of his
warning—and thus to understand adequately the context in which
the mission is to be carried out—it is well to probe beneath the
surface of the words *world* and *religion,* to assess the nature of the
anticipated hostility and to consider the appropriate attitude of the
church as it confronts that antipathy.

In a remarkably compact and precise segment of *Dialogue with
the World,* J. G. Davies makes a very helpful study of the meaning of
the noun *world* as it is used in the New Testament. Noting that the
word is deceptively complex, he points out that *kosmos,* only one of
several Greek words translated as *world* in English, has as many as
four distinct meanings. It may designate personal adornment, such as
a lady's hair style (1 Pet. 3:3); the inhabited world of men (Rom.
1:8); the sum total of creation (Col. 1:16f.); or the organized forces
of paganism (1 John 5:19). The first two meanings are basically
neutral in shading. The third is essentially positive and good, because
it is related to God's creativity. The last is fundamentally negative,
since it represents a methodical concentration of evil.[1]

Because of its varied meanings, the word *world* in the New
Testament should always be read with an eye to the sense the author
intended in a particular place. Similarly, the reader should never
permit one application of the word to spill over and dilute or
displace its other meanings. The use of *kosmos, world,* in the
farewell discourses is a case in point. Here, as in most of the rest of
Johannine literature and in many places in the Pauline epistles, the
meaning of the word is the fourth one on Davies' list: "human
society as organized under the power of evil."[2] This rendition of
world is appropriate in the context of Jesus' last conversations with
his disciples and in the light of the fourth evangelist's experience

with early resistance to the gospel. But in order to appreciate the full biblical attitude toward the world, this Johannine use must be balanced with more positive applications of the word. To universalize this single, negative meaning, as some Christians have done at various points in history, produces a warped theological view of the world as something strenuously to be shunned as totally corrupt. Of course Christians are to take the power of evil seriously and to stand steadfastly against it, but this does not require wholesale condemnation of or separation from the world, as it is broadly understood.

When Jesus predicted that his followers would be banned from the synagogues and hounded and killed by religious fanatics, he was implicitly drawing a fine but definite distinction between religion and the kingdom which he proclaimed and inaugurated. *Religion*, in this sense, is a narrow, limited word. It may refer to a purely finite system of values constructed out of a people's search for the truth about their world. It may signify a particular human response to the revelation of a god or gods. More likely, it reflects an ordering which consciously combines both mortal "upreach" and divine "downreach." Judaism, for example, the religion with which Jesus was most familiar, is a profound arrangement of what a certain community of men have come to believe is the God-revealed truth about the nature of things. But because it is a human response it is fallible, open to error and corruption. Neither Judaism nor Christianity nor any other religion can be identified *per se* with the truth. Neither Judaism nor Christianity nor any other religion is ever entirely free from base motives or deplorable actions, for religious men are as much a part of the world as non-religious. They too may come under the sway of evil. Tragic though it may be, it is not particularly surprising, therefore, that Judaism in league with paganism condemned a Jesus or that Christianity in league with paganism condoned a Hitler.

But the concept of the kingdom, which Jesus introduced, is far more than a high human arrangement of perceived or received truth. It represents the objective, authoritative reign of God over his creation. The inauguration of the kingdom has been announced. It is operative now and fully accessible to mankind, though its perfection and completion will take effect beyond time and human history. Men and women may choose to become citizens of this kingdom by their own free will, but they do not create it and it is not in their power to alter or control it—or, perhaps, even to understand it completely. Because it is beyond human tampering and tinkering it is absolutely distinct from mere religion. As in the case of Christianity, religion may speak of the kingdom—indeed shout about it—and seek to point men toward it. But no religion, not even Christianity, may be identified with the kingdom of God.

Having briefly explored the meanings hidden within the terms *world* and *religion,* we may now turn to examine the dark recesses of the hostility Jesus predicted would proceed from the hearts of both worldlings and religionists. What are the dynamics of this antipathy?

As we have noted, one way of defining the world—and *only* one way—is by its ability to hate. If God is absolute love, then the world, as "society organized under the power of evil," is unmitigated hate. And what does hate hate most? Love, its antagonist. People who personify the abstract idea *world* hate God because of the demands his unsentimental love places on them. Perverse people want a tame, indulgent household god that can be kept on the mantlepiece or pressed between the leaves of the family Bible and taken down or trotted out in cases of emergency or, far less frequently, on occasions of celebration. But God refuses to be domesticated by man, even as his kingdom refuses to be captured by religion. His absolute supremacy and total independence, his universal love and will to wholeness, contradict and threaten the insatiable human desire to control everything for self-indulgent ends. So the world hates him—or, more safely and surely, it hates those who are clearly committed to him.

The ministry of Jesus of Nazareth had a way of concentrating and intensifying the basic hatred of the world. Because he was the wholly responsive person, he revealed more completely than anyone before or since how God's will is meant to operate in men. As the first strip of new wallpaper pasted over the old shows how faded and soiled the previous covering had become, so Jesus' fresh, full response had the inevitable effect of exposing the pettiness and evil of man's self-will. It is an unsettling experience for self-indulgent men to be confronted with perfect love. They may try to hide from that love. They may change in response to it. Or they may openly or secretly declare a war of hate against it. And hate, of course, is a starting-point of murder, even murder lightly disguised as legal and justified execution.

Since the followers of Jesus carry on his ministry, the hatred which had been focussed on him is now turned toward them. Indeed that hostility is a sign of discipleship, for "a servant is not greater than his master" (John 15:20). It is the disciples' mutual indwelling with their Lord which guarantees that they will receive the same treatment, and the extent of that treatment will be determined only by the limitations of their own faithfulness. Jesus Christ has drawn his disciples out of the world's field of gravity and into his own. His gospel presents a radically different orientation from the standards of the world. If his people make a proper response to the gospel, if they speak and act clearly and if the world understands what they intend to convey, then opposition, hostility, conflict are inescapable.

In the opening pages of *The Secular City,* Harvey Cox appears to contradict the inevitability of hostility and conflict in the modern, secular world when he quite accurately observes that the

> forces of secularization have no serious interest in persecuting religion. Secularization simply bypasses and undercuts religion and goes on to other things. It has relativized religious world-views and thus rendered them innocuous. Religion has been privatized. It has been accepted as the peculiar prerogative and point of view of a particular person or group. Secularization has accomplished what fire and chain could not: It has convinced the believer that he *could* be wrong, and persuaded the devotee that there are more important things than dying for the faith.[3]

Those words, in fact, strengthen the argument. For where there is no conflict with the world, as may be the case in some sections of secular civilization, then it is certain that the Christian church has sold out to the surrounding culture and has consequently failed in its calling. To one degree or another it has been seduced by the temptations of religion and has betrayed its commitment to proclaim the controversial kingdom of God. William Temple once wrote, "That disciple or that church which finds that all men speak well of him or it, has cause for anxiety,"[4] to which could be consistently added: and that disciple or that church which is ignored by the world has equal cause for concern.

We have acknowledged that even those who do believe in God may hate and destroy others who truly seek to conform to his will, for no man—religious or otherwise—is free from the taint of sin. Manifestations of this "holy" hostility are found throughout history.

According to the Mishnah, a Jew had the right to kill a man caught in blasphemy. Thus when the leaders of Judaism condemned

Jesus, the one whom the prophets had foretold, it was done to protect the people of God from a blasphemer. There was hostility among Jesus' own disciples. Judas betrayed him for reasons that were never clear, but which certainly involved a conflicting interpretation of the role of the movement Jesus led. Later Saul of Tarsus gained a reputation throughout the Eastern Mediterranean world as a fanatical persecutor of early Christians. To be sure, that grisly experience began to reshape his life and ultimately altered the course of modern history. But the enormity of what that great man of religion did cannot be evaded. As C. L. Rieu notes,

> there is a harshness and even a brutality about Paul. Most critics appear to think that his own trials, scourgings, and final martyrdom make up for his original persecuting, whipping, and imprisoning of Christians. So they do, in a way, and he himself regarded his sufferings as retribution in kind. Nevertheless the deeds could not be undone and he did them: in his full and developed manhood (for Jews did not enter on public life till they were 30) he indulged in brutal persecution that reminds one of the Inquisition. He used violence on people because their beliefs were not his own—yet.[5]

The Bishops at the Council of Constance, with all of their mixed motives, surely believed that they were protecting the sanctity of the church's doctrine when they put the Bohemian reformer Jan Hus to the torch. In America today there are certain kinds of Christians who harass, maim, or kill both fellow Christians and non-Christians whose only heresy is to seek justice for the dispossessed. It was not without insight, then, that Jesus cautioned his disciples that many of their tormentors will think that they are doing God a favor, a grand delusion which makes religious persecutors the most relentless of all.

Faced with hostility from both secular and sacred segments of society, faithful Christians are tempted to avoid the direct and painful confrontation discipleship often demands. As I suggested in the last chapter, there are two easily identifiable escape hatches (among several other less obvious ones) commonly used to elude conflict with the world. Both are somewhat related to the main task and can be readily justified by Scripture, which makes them very convenient outlets indeed.

One exit leads through the corridors of withdrawal. By turning into an updated version of a hermit the individual Christian can easily and comfortably be isolated from the conflict. Along this escape route the emphasis is placed on the inner life, on piety, on keeping oneself close to God and unspotted by the world.

The other exit lies down the path of worldliness. There is much talk in Christian circles these days of letting the world set the agenda for the church. This is excellent. But the tendency for timid Christians is, as Davies puts it, to "accept the agenda of the twentieth century without any alteration, so that they merely endorse the *status quo* and deny the revolutionary nature of their faith."[6] Many Christians are heading down the road toward holy worldliness today, as a rightful reaction to a former period of insulation. The difficulty comes in knowing just where to turn off the path or to halt the journey before it becomes a flight from conflict, an escape from responsibility.

God's mission cannot be served effectively if his partners are totally removed from the world or if their identification with the world is so complete that they are virtually indistinguishable from it. Jesus was aware of the problem and gave it a central place in his great summary prayer for wholeness at the end of the farewell discourses:

> I have delivered thy word to them, and the world hates them because they are strangers in the world, as I am. I pray thee, not to take them out of the world, but to keep them from the evil one. They are strangers in the world, as I am. Consecrate them by the truth; thy word is truth. As thou hast sent me into the world, I have sent them into the world, and for their sake I now consecrate myself, that they too may be consecrated by the truth. (17:14-19)

He asked his Father not to draw his disciples out of the world, but to prevent their propensity to escape merely because the world regards them as strangers. He also implored God to keep them from the spell of "the evil one," from being seduced by the ever-shifting standards of the world. He prayed that they would be given the kind of perspective and balance which comes through knowing and accepting the truth. His concern was that the middle ground be found on which his disciples could stand with independence and objectivity and yet with relevance to the world into which he was sending them.

The paradox of the Christian life is that the followers of that way

are meant to be in the world but not of it. Since this is the only
world into which Christians are born, they are intended to be
completely at home in it and profoundly in love with it. Any *no*
Christians may ultimately say to the world, as Hans Schultz reminds
us,

> will only carry weight if there is a fundamental *yes* at its heart,
> a *yes* springing from the deepest fraternal partnership with all
> other human beings no matter how different in outlook, faith
> or colour.[7]

At the same time, Christians are utterly uncomfortable in this world,
for their faith in Christ has given them the credentials of citizenship
in another country. This is doubtless an underlying cause of the
world's hatred, for it begrudges Christians their divided loyalty. Just
as Jason, Silas, and Paul were excoriated for allegedly flouting the
emperor's laws and asserting that there is a rival king, namely Jesus
(Acts 17:5-9), so their successors bear the same accusation by the
men of the world.

Although Christians must not allow the world's hatred to drive
them into isolation, they do have a distinct life of their own. In
What in the World? Colin Williams explains how delicate an
adjustment to living this requires. The way of the world is not the
way of Christ, he says, so when Christians

> gather to acknowledge Christ's Lordship over his creation and
> to witness to him, they find that they are in tension with the
> way of the world. But this does not mean that the church has
> a separate sphere: a separate segment of life from the segments
> for which the other institutions of the world have responsibil-
> ity. The separate life of the church is in the world and for the
> world; and the life of the church is meant to be seen by men as
> the sign of Christ's purpose for all life: as the "firstfruits" of
> Christ's redeeming purpose for his whole creation.[8]

How to discover the line of demarcation between these two
aspects of the Christian calling—ministry in behalf of the world and
allegiance to the kingdom—is one of the most pressing and difficult
problems facing the church in this (or any) age. Today it is reflected
especially in the doubt, frustration, and ambivalence of clergy in
every church, many of whom are leaving ecclesiastical employment
in order to seek greater relevance for their ministries in secular

positions. It is also mirrored in the lingering uncertainty felt by every Christian denomination about the church's role in the social revolutions of our time. Jesus offered no easy solution to the perplexity. He merely enunciated the double principle of being in the world but not of it. For he saw—as we must come to see—that no pattern is suitable for every person, for every group, for every situation, for every era. Each citizen of the kingdom needs to search out the frontier himself—either alone or in exploratory parties—using whatever points of reference the Christian tradition provides. Through that endeavor, which probably lasts a lifetime, he may come to accept what is for him a valid set of boundary lines.

IV

THE MANNER OF THE MISSION

During supper, Jesus, well aware that the Father had entrusted everything to him, and that he had come from God and was going back to God, rose from table, laid aside his garments, and taking a towel, tied it round him. Then he poured water into a basin, and began to wash his disciples' feet and to wipe them with the towel.

When it was Simon Peter's turn, Peter said to him, "You, Lord, washing my feet?" "If I do not wash you," Jesus replied, "you are not in fellowship with me." "Then, Lord," said Simon Peter, "not my feet only; wash my hands and head as well!"

Jesus said, "A man who has bathed needs no further washing; he is altogether clean; and you are clean, though not every one of you." He added the words "not every one of you" because he knew who was going to betray him.

After washing their feet and taking his garments again, he sat down. "Do you understand," he asked, "what I have done for you? You call me 'Master' and 'Lord', and rightly so, for that is what I am. Then if I, your Lord and Master, have washed your feet, you also ought to wash one another's feet. I have set you an example: you are to do as I have done for you. In very

*truth I tell you, a servant is not greater than his master, nor a
messenger than the one who sent him. If you know this, happy
are you if you act upon it. "*

John 13:3-27(NEB)

The disciples had gathered in a second-story room in Jerusalem
for what would turn out to be their last fellowship meal with Jesus.
Although the other Gospels are silent on the point, Luke's version of
the event records that when supper was well along, an argument
broke out among them about their rank in the kingdom (Luke
22:24-27). This was apparently a renewal of the petulant,
thoroughly human rivalry and speculation to which Jesus had
deliberately addressed himself before (Matt. 18:1-5; Mark 9:33-37;
Luke 9:46-48). But the disciples couldn't seem to leave the subject
alone. The recurrence of the dispute on this particular occasion, the
significance of which they had not yet fathomed, may have touched
off the parable that Jesus proceeded to act out in their midst.

He realized that this would be his last chance to clarify the
meaning of God's mission and the manner in which it was to be
accomplished. Being "well aware that the Father had entrusted
everything to him" he knew that he had to make his role and the
role of the disciples perfectly transparent. Words alone would not be
sufficient. A demonstration was necessary. So he got up from the
table, stripped off his clothes, wrapped a towel around himself, put
water in a basin and began to wash the feet of his followers.

In the ancient Middle East foot washing was a regular part of
good hospitality. While a guest may have fully bathed before
departing for a dinner party, on the way to his host's house his feet
would become soiled again by the dust of the road. A thoughtful
and proper first-century host would have provided his arriving guests
with water, a basin, a towel and probably a servant to do the actual
labor. If the householder were prosperous and had a number of
servants or slaves, the most menial of them would have been assigned
this unpleasant duty.

By performing a task relegated to the most subservient slave,
Jesus was acting out a lesson in humility. He was showing his
disputing disciples what authority and dignity in the kingdom really
involve: "the highest among you must bear himself like the
youngest, the chief of you like a servant" (Luke 22:26). However,
the manner in which this incident developed and the occasion on

which it took place give the foot washing more than a mere moral significance. Two further interpretations must be drawn from this remarkable act to complete the picture Jesus was attempting to make clear.

When Jesus said to Peter, "You do not understand now what I am doing, but one day you will," he was placing his action within the framework of his impending doom. The first interpretation of this acted parable, therefore, concerns the meaning of Jesus' passion and death.

The new order being inaugurated by Christ depended on his complete constancy and reliability, on his humiliation to the very point of extinction. Jesus had counseled closely with the twelve; he had instructed a wider band of followers; he had preached to the multitudes. But with all of that, he was not primarily a teacher. He was a rescuer. And his rescue operation depended on discipline and obedience, as well as good timing. Since a rescuer primarily is one who acts rather than speaks, all his efforts at verbal communication were related to and in support of his essential action. P. T. Forsyth got to the heart of the matter when he described Jesus as the one "whose pulpit was His Cross, whose Cross made disciples apostles, in whose Cross God first preached to the world, whose preaching from the Cross has done for the world what all of His discourses—even His discourses—failed to do.[1] By washing their feet Jesus was trying to convey to his disciples that they were to look for the meaning of his mission not in his words but in his actions—especially in the culminating action which would begin with his imminent betrayal. The parable he played out was a prefiguration of his death.

Long before John F. Kennedy uttered memorable words of somewhat similar syntax but entirely different purport, William Temple commented on his portion of the Fourth Gospel by advising in effect: Ask not what you can do for God but what God would do for you.[2] That terse suggestion points toward a second meaning Jesus intended to impart by washing his disciples' feet.

He wanted to demonstrate that man's creative partnership with God begins with learning to receive from the one who is greater than we. This is not easy for self-contained, self-reliant human beings to accept. Simon Peter, who was so independent and strong-willed that he was nicknamed "the rock," quickly recognized the implications of Jesus' action. It was inconsistent with his view of the order of things to allow his master to humiliate himself, and so with characteristic impulsiveness he blurted out, "I will never let you wash my feet." Though Peter might have been ready to give his own life for Jesus at that moment, he couldn't seem to accept a simple and symbolic act of self-offering from him.

Twentieth-century American Christians should have little trouble identifying with Peter, for our perspective is remarkably close to his. Basically we are givers rather than receivers, aggressive-autonomous types rather than passive-dependent. Despite unsettling signs of inner weakness and decay, we are still governed today by an expansive mood of largesse based on abundance and power. We are not in a receptive temper.

Politically we are proud of our self-generating, self-perpetuating, self-sufficient form of democracy, the ideological key to which is labeled The Declaration of *Independence.* Although no thoughtful American wishes to denigrate the dignity of that document, the high resolve it represents does sometimes descend into a naive and righteous kind of nationalism marked by the tendency to think that one's own point-of-view, one's own manner of operation, one's own best interests automatically coincide with those of every other country. With a mixture of pride, gratitude, and condescension we desire to share our achievements—up to a point—with others. Such an attitude is never an announced principle of foreign policy, but it conveys itself in many ways nonetheless—sometimes subtly, sometimes obviously. It is a great temptation for very powerful nations.

In more personal terms our stereotype of success centers on the person who started with nothing and made it to the top by applying his talents to every opportunity, apparently without the help of anyone else. We call him "a self-made man." The goal of all his efforts has been to make himself independently wealthy. Ecclesiastically we have designed our missionary strategy so that the aim of all dependent groups of Christians (commonly called missions) is to become self-supporting, self-governing churches, as if the pinnacle of Christian maturity were self-reliance. Accepting responsibility for oneself as a nation, a person, or a Christian community is, of course, an essential part of maturation. But the desire for total independence in any of these areas of life leads towards the wasteland of utter self-centeredness, where the creative possibilities men are meant to share with God dry up and disappear.

"If I do not wash you," Jesus replied to Peter's demurral, "you are not in fellowship with me," for there is no place in Christian discipleship for those who have not been cleansed by Christ and acknowledged it. To permit him to do this for us is to enter into a relationship of reciprocal surrender and trust, of mutual indwelling, in which pride is exchanged for partnership and privilege for servitude. The significance of this somewhat startling concept of divine-human relationship based on mutuality is vast. As Harvey Cox suggests, it may just introduce estranged contemporary man to God again, not as a remote and austere authority figure this time, but as a close collaborator in a common task. Asking himself if this is farfetched, Cox replies,

> Recent discussions of the concept of the covenant in the Old Testament suggest it means that Yahweh was willing to stoop so low as to work in tandem with man, to work on a team no matter how poorly the human partner was working out. Whether or not this is true, it can certainly be said that in Jesus of Nazareth God did show that He was willing to take man's side of the unfulfilled covenant, to become the junior partner in the asymmetric relationship. It is not demeaning to suggest that the notions of teamwork and partnership need to be explored much more in our conceptualization of God. He who is "high and lifted up" suggests in the life of Jesus that he is willing to put himself in the position of working within a group, of washing his fellows' feet and of needing someone to carry his cross. What seems at first sight irreverence may be closer to the heart of the self-humbling truth of God than we imagine.[3]

After he had completed his quick exchange of comments with Peter and finished washing the feet of the rest around the room, Jesus took pains to explain further what he had just done. He wanted to leave nothing to their imaginations, nothing to chance: "Then if I, your Lord and Master, have washed your feet, you also ought to wash one another's feet. I have set you an example: you are to do as I have done for you." Here Jesus seems to be giving instructions that pertain especially to the inner life of the latent church: honor and serve each other. Among its other functions and responsibilities, he implied, the community of faith is meant to be a scale model of what life in the kingdom is like, to demonstrate in small compass what human relationships should be in full size.

In Japan there is an ancient cultural phenomenon known as *On*. As well as a foreigner can understand and explain it, *On* operates as a buffer to protect people from the intolerable position of becoming excessively indebted to one another. According to the *On* axiom, one person inflicts a great disservice on another if he comes to his aid in any special way, for the rendering of unusual service places the recipient under a tremendous obligation to repay the deed. The greater the help, the more massive the burden of repayment becomes. Even today in Japan people will pass by a badly injured person on the street, not necessarily because they are hard-hearted, but because, according to the classical principle of *On*, they do the victim a greater kindness by not putting him in their debt.

The formal mechanism of *On* is gradually disappearing from the Japanese scene, probably due in large measure to Western influence. But the human sickness behind it is as endemic as ever—in Japan and everywhere else. Nothing could be farther from the spirit of the Christian gospel. The *On*-like desire not to be beholden to anyone is as narrow and dangerous a way to travel as that other one-way street of personal relationships: to constantly take from others and give nothing in return. If the church is supposed to be a model of human community, then it should be a context within which men may discover—and not without pain and conflict—what it means to receive as well as to give. In nurturing such an attitude of interdependence among men, the church will also be demonstrating the Christian's love for, commitment to, and mutual interaction with the senior partner in the divine-human enterprise of renewing and perfecting creation.

Jesus' instructions were well heard and well heeded by the fledgling church. Outsiders who observed their fellowship noted immediately the different quality it conveyed. "See how these Christians love one another," the Roman world commented, sometimes in jealous accusation, sometimes in amazed admiration.[4] Many of those impressed were inevitably drawn into the Christian community—as converts from the grasping standards of the world to a life of mutual sharing. As a sign and seal of this interdependent inner life, early Christians retained the Lord's small sacrament of foot washing as a liturgical act. In some parts of the church the custom has continued down to the present. Here and there foot washing is being restored to a place of importance, perhaps as a harbinger of a new style of Christian life. The two most recent popes, John XXIII and Paul VI, have themselves engaged in liturgical foot washing on Maundy Thursday, not only before marble altars among fastidious functionaries but also out in the streets of Rome among the poor of their diocese. By this dramatic action these two quite different pontiffs have shown that there is more than an inward, ceremonial significance to the foot washing. There is an outward, missionary meaning too, for Jesus exchanged his scepter and crown for a basin and towel, and abandoned his throne for a cross, not only for the sake of his own small company of companions but for the entire world.

Having counseled the disciples to wash one another's feet, Jesus rushes on in the very next breath to give his acted parable the widest possible meaning: "In very truth I tell you, a servant is not greater than his master, *nor a messenger than the one who sent him.*" In that key sentence John attributes one very revealing word to Jesus. The word is *messenger—apostolos* in Greek—and its importance lies in the fact that it appears only this one time in the Fourth Gospel. The evangelist usually uses *the twelve* or *disciples* to describe Jesus' closest companions. But here he clearly wants to transform the communal (servant-master) context of the foot washing into a universal expression by linking it directly with the message to be carried to the world by the young apostolic church. The outward thrust of what Jesus manifested in the upper room is essential, explicit, clear.

One worldwide family of churches has recently been trying to rethink and restate its calling in contemporary society. Many of its earliest conclusions are summed up in a document in which this single sentence has a pivotal position: "The Church exists to witness, to obey and to serve."[5] Although it comes last in the list, the crucial, operative infinitive is "to serve." What does it mean merely "to witness"? Is it a matter of conjuring up the right words at the right time? But words alone are really rather empty in the end. If Jesus had talked about the need for consistent self-giving but avoided the cross as the consequence of his dependability, all of his parables and preachments would have a hollow sound today. What does it mean simply "to obey"? We need to know what the orders are and, more decisively, how we are to obey them. Ultimately the keystone to obedient Christian witness, as a person or a community, is to engage in what has been called "disinterested service."

On the surface the term "disinterested service" seems to imply a kind of cold, impersonal, detached dispensing of charity. In its deeper meaning it expresses what is involved in losing oneself in a ministry in behalf of others without counting the cost in terms of sacrifice or calculating the response in terms of gain or loss. It signifies doing a job because it needs to be done, not because it will increase the size or the prestige of the church. The concept of "disinterested service" may be sharpened by comparing slogans used by two service-oriented groups, one not specifically Christian, the other an official part of the church. A large international organization composed of business and professional men has as one of its two mottoes, "He profits most who serves the best." There is no doubt that a greater spirit of service is needed in shops and offices today, but the motive to serve, as expressed in this particular maxim, is obviously tied to the desire for personal gain. The admonition may have good effect, but it would not seem to produce *disinterested* service.[6] There is a religious order in the Roman Catholic Church which is primarily devoted to interpreting the Catholic faith to non-Catholics. While a passion for proselytes may be hidden somewhere in the picture, this group's self-description comes closer to the concept of disinterested service: "A community of people who serve God by serving those not of their church." That depiction could well apply to the entire Christian household.

When Jesus washed the feet of his friends he was actually doing the work of a slave, a person who had no status in society at all, at least as rank is normally measured by the world. Is there a clue here for the church? The comments of two contemporary thinkers, who happen to be critics of Christianity, confirm and expand the intriguing idea that the church is really meant to be a society of slaves.

In his book *The Secular Promise,* Martin Jarrett-Kerr refers to a criticism made by the humanist professor J. C. Flugel that Christianity fostered a deplorable divorce between ethics and politics by failing to provide outlets for the energies of aggressive extroverts or positive social and political goals. Fr. Jarrett-Kerr goes on to note that Flugel and other men of action see Christianity "as representing nothing but a 'slave morality'—an interesting recurrence in the twentieth century of the reproach levelled against it by Roman civilization in the second and third."[7] "Slave morality," in this instance, means the subservient, unquestioning acceptance of things as they are, which belongs to a mind conditioned by living precariously perched on the lowest step of civilization's staircase. That view of slavery in the Roman Empire is, of course, oversimplified. There were surprisingly large numbers of slaves who were clever, astutue, and highly literate and who had greater (though perhaps indirect) influence on men and affairs than their lack of official status would indicate. But the Christian stance that the "slave morality" aspersion suggests has interesting possibilities.

Roger Garaudy, the leading French Marxist philosopher, reads history in a rather different way. In his perceptive and appreciatively critical analysis of Christianity *From Anathema to Dialogue* he writes:

> In ... putting the accent on human initiative, many Christians have experienced the return to what is basic as a return to primitive Christianity. Passing over the many centuries of the Church's "Constantinian" tradition (a tradition constituted by close connections with the ruling classes and the established power, and by the assimilation of Greco-Latin ideologies with their hierarchical conceptions of the world), many Christians today are attempting to rediscover the apocalyptic tradition of primitive Christianity, the tradition of an age when Christianity was a "slaves" religion, a protest, however weak, against the established order, and a hope for the coming of the Kingdom on earth as in heaven, when Christianity had not yet become an ideology of imperial justification and of resignation....[8]

In contrast to his fellow humanist, Prof. Garaudy sees early Christianity as an awakening of the masses to their power. He hopes that the current movements of renewal in the church reflect an attempt to recover Christianity's early apocalyptic tradition, the drive to bring about change in history. As "a 'slaves' religion," Garaudy believes, authentic (apocalyptic) Christianity is a potential revolutionary force against all forms of entrenched inhumanity and injustice.

What is called for in the church today is a fusion of those characteristics of slavery which were touched on negatively by Flugel and positively by Garaudy. The church as a community of slaves is intended to be an agent of revolution. Revolution indicates change, and change for the better is an essential part of the continuation of creation in which God and man cooperate. But the church as a community of slaves is also meant to have no possessions of its own, to work in habitations which are not its own, to have no power, no status, except the power and status which belong to a truly free humanity. The revolution to which the church is called is to win everything for mankind and nothing for itself. This is what the slave-like action of washing feet ultimately means.

An element of realism enters when it is noted that John's account of the foot washing is enclosed by references to the betrayal of Jesus. The evangelist begins his depiction of the event by remarking that "The devil had already put it into the mind of Judas son of Simon Iscariot to betray him" (13:2). And after the narrative ends he records that "Jesus exclaimed in deep agitation of spirit, 'In truth, in very truth I tell you, one of you is going to betray me' " (13:21). Since the slave-like service suggested by the foot washing does not conform to the criteria of the world, it is always undertaken at the risk of ridicule, misunderstanding, and treachery. More than ordinary human resources are needed to bring it to good effect.

V

POWER FOR THE MISSION

"If you love me you will obey my commands; and I will ask the Father, and he will give you another to be your Advocate, who will be with you for ever—the Spirit of truth. The world cannot receive him because the world neither sees nor knows him; but you know him, because he dwells with you and is in you. I will not leave you bereft; I am coming back to you. In a little while the world will see me no longer, but you will know that I am in my Father, and you in me and I in you. The man who has received my commands and obeys them—he it is who loves me; and he who loves me will be loved by my Father; and I will love him and disclose myself to him."

Judas asked him—the other Judas, not Iscariot—"Lord, what can have happened, that you mean to disclose yourself to us alone and not to the world?" Jesus replied, "Anyone who loves me will heed what I say; then my Father will love him and we will come to him and make our dwelling with him; but he who does not love me does not heed what I say. And the word you hear is not mine: it is the word of the Father who sent me. I have told you all this while I am still here with you; but your Advocate, the Holy Spirit whom the Father will send in my name, will teach you everything, and will call to mind all that I have told you."

John 14:15-26(NEB)

As we observed at the outset, the worldwide church is struggling with a vast ambivalence about its place in God's mission. There are doubts and disagreements within the Christian community that didn't exist in previous periods of missionary work and certainly not 1900, 200, or even 50 years ago. Because of the peculiar circumstances of our time, large segments of the church are raising questions about its calling that haven't been asked with such searching perplexity before. What unique claim does Christianity present modern men? What special roles may the other great religions have in God's mission? Does the competence of secular man erase the need for any, or even for every, religious enterprise? What is the nature of conversion? Is it in fact the central task of the church? How is the authentic action of God discerned in the social and political aspects of life? What is the church's connection to it? How do Christians make a valid and vigorous response to God's call to mission without becoming so preoccupied with local problems that the broader issues are overlooked, or without becoming so immersed in far-flung activities that they become an escape from the disturbing challenges close at hand?

That such questions and many more are being raised and argued about is a sign of health within the body of faith. Not only are the issues important in themselves, they also reflect a readiness among Christians to react in new ways to fresh demands placed upon the church by God and history—or, more accurately, by God *in* history. But behind these particular questions and at the heart of the wider ambivalence of our age lies the most basic problem of all, the problem of obedience. Assuming that with ears attuned to the times Christians do hear God's summons to partnership, how do they obey with perception and constancy? Exhortations to obedience have always found their place in the writing and speaking of missionary leaders. But the whiplash of "obedience" in mission is no more effective or meaningful in the long run than the goad of the "ought" in ethics. Obedience to the will of God is the *result* of faithful human response not the *source* of it. It is the acceleration of the vehicle not its fuel or engine. The central question, therefore, has to be this: How is the spark ignited that causes an explosion of power which, if properly harnessed, propels servants of the gospel into every conceivable situation far and near?

An answer to the dilemma of obedience is regularly signaled

throughout the farewell discourses by the skillful repetition of
pointed references to the promised gift of the Spirit. Like Pavlov's
bells, a series of so-called "paraclete sayings" are sounded periodi-
cally in Jesus' final instructions, as if he were deliberately trying to
condition his disciples to be especially alert and receptive. One of
the longest and most revealing of these five predictions of the
coming of the paraclete is recorded in John 14:15-26. Three major
points emerge from that passage, which is reproduced at the head of
this chapter.

First, no man can consistently obey the directives "to go" or "to
serve" or any other command without love. A person cannot obey
Jesus Christ unless he loves him. Conversely, those who do love him
will have no trouble in obeying him. Likewise, men cannot
adequately serve others unless they love them. But if this is true,
then the prerequisite of love becomes the greatest commandment of
all. When one of the Pharisees asked Jesus, " 'Master, which is the
greatest commandment in the Law?' He answered, 'Love the Lord
your God with all your heart, with all your soul, with all your mind,'
and 'Love your neighbor as yourself' " (Matt. 22:37-39). Throughout the farewell discourses he made the point repeatedly to his own
disciples as well. "I give you a new commandment: love one
another" (John 13:34). "This is my commandment: love one
another, as I have loved you" (John 15:12).

As always, the law in any form is impossible to observe fully with
human resources alone. To put the love-obedience coefficient into
operation, therefore, an enabling power is needed. Jesus, according
to John, summed it all up practically in one breath, "If you love me
you will obey my commands; and I will ask the Father, and he will
give you another to be your Advocate, who will be with you
forever—the Spirit of truth." A tremendous amount seems to hang
on that single—almost ambiguous—transitional word *and.* Does the
gift of the Spirit of God come as the result of a response of
love-obedience, or does it come as the motivating power for those
who seek to love and obey? The last verse in this segment of the
discourses makes it clear. "The Holy Spirit whom the Father will
send . . . will teach you everything." He will lead, guide, train, and
tutor us in the way to go.

If the root problem is lack of love—for God, for his Son, for the
world, for ourselves too—it can be reversed only through personal
relationships. We do not love someone we do not know, except in

the most abstract way. We cannot love Jesus Christ and obey him if we have not known him. The disciples had the advantage of knowing him directly during his earthly ministry. But what about us latter-day Christians? How do we come to know and serve him? We gain a remote appreciation of him through the New Testament, of course, but in order to come alive, that second-hand knowledge must be confirmed by the power of the Spirit working through other persons who mediate in their lives the same quality of love he manifested in his life.

The enabling power, then, is a personal power. The somewhat sterile terms *spirit* or *paraclete (paracletos)* are often substituted with *advocate* (NEB), *comforter* (KJV), *counselor* (RSV), *helper, guardian*—all of which are thoroughly personal descriptions. It is this personal paraclete who continues to reveal the very being of Christ and to communicate his sustained presence. Jesus promised that the Father would send the Spirit in *his name,* as the extension of his personhood: " . . . when your advocate has come, whom I will send you from the Father—the Spirit of truth that issues from the Father—he will bear witness to *me*" (John 15:26). Ultimately, therefore, it is no ethereal potency to whom we respond, but rather the living Spirit of Jesus, the Christ. He is the enabling power, though we ordinarily meet him and respond to him only through the remarkable chain reaction of human encounter.

The Pentecostal experience of the earliest disciples themselves illustrates the need for this enabling power. Even those who had known Jesus best and had shared the most important part of his life among men couldn't continue to respond effectively to him after his execution. They were a shattered, scattered lot. They needed the free gift of his continued presence in order that their love-evoked obedience could be kept alive. When the existence of his Spirit in their midst became evident to them, dramatized and authenticated by the Pentecostal symbols of wind and fire, they were changed from a confused and protective band of frightened men and women into an extroverted revolutionary force which would help to shape the course of human history.

A second point in the paraclete pronouncements is introduced by the question asked of Jesus by the less well known of the two Judases among the disciples. In twentieth-century terms the loyal Judas was asking: Is this personal, enabling power—the Spirit of Christ—only available and operable through the closed community of faith, or is he accessible to all men? He was slightly bewildered and disturbed—rightfully and perceptively so—because Jesus seemed to be describing the rest of the world as territory sealed off from the operation of the Spirit. To Judas, who may have remembered the words of the prophet Joel, such a suggestion was clearly nonscriptural.

The world to which John's Jesus referred, of course, was the Johannine world of organized evil that deliberately shuts itself off from the creative power of God. His answer to Judas clarifies what he meant: *"Anyone* who loves me will heed what I say; then my Father will love him, and we will come to him and make our dwelling with him." The Spirit works within *any* man who responds to the reality that Jesus represents and reflects, whether that man names Jesus as Lord or not. The test of discipleship is met not by making promises or assuming titles but by responding to the promptings of the Spirit and claiming partnership with God by being obedient in love. Jesus illustrated this perfectly on another occasion with the parable of the two sons, one of whom told his father he wouldn't go into the vineyard to work but did and the other who promised he would and didn't (Matt. 21:28-32).

As I have already suggested, Jesus uses his repeated references to the paraclete to drive home a third point: he wanted to create among these chosen few a sense of expectancy toward the unimagined power about to be released in and among them, as if his Spirit would be discerned only if his coming were anticipated. "The Father ... will give you another ... ," he told them. "I have told you all this while I am still here with you; but ... the Holy Spirit whom the Father will send ... will call to mind all that I have told you," he concluded, knowing that much would be forgotten in the confusion to follow. That he only partly succeeded in his conditioning process and that he was right in his prediction of amnesia is confirmed by the almost uncanny inability of his followers to recognize him when he appeared to them after his resurrection. Mary Magdalene thought he was the gardener until he spoke her name (John 20:14-16). Cleopas and his companion failed at first to grasp who he was on the road to Emmaus (Luke 24:15). Those who were fishing with Simon Peter off the Galilean shore didn't recognize him until he suggested how they could increase their catch (John 21:4-7). Thomas wouldn't believe that it was Jesus standing before him until he put his hands into his wounds (John 20:24-29).

After centuries of rehearsing the experiences of the first disciples, Christians, for the most part, still haven't got the message. If contemporary disciples are going to do anything about redeeming this age of doubt and confusion, then they require nothing more urgently than a corporate mood of Pentecostal expectancy, a readiness to anticipate, to search for, and to validate every movement of the Spirit of Christ in their midst and in the world at large.

The greatest missionary certainty and vitality appears to exist today, at least in terms of personal conversion, among those Christians called conservative evangelicals. These churchmen, who are biblical literalists for the most part, do not believe in wasting much time disputing the authenticity of the ending of Mark's Gospel. They take the dominical command precisely at its word and "go forth to every part of the world and proclaim the Good News to the whole creation" (Mark 16:15). Within this part of Christianity the most spectacular growth is taking place through the Pentecostal movement, particularly in Latin America. While arguments may be leveled against certain aspects of the theology of Pentecostalists and while regret may be expressed over their disproportionate stress on personal religion to the neglect of social concerns, their vitality, spontaneity and almost complete reliance upon unpaid leadership command tremendous respect. Their experience is bringing pressure on other Christians to reexamine their presuppositions and re-evaluate their missionary methods. It is highly significant that the central motivating force of the Pentecostal movement springs not out of a static biblical literalism, but out of another kind of fundamentalism. As their name implies, they rely totally on the power of the Spirit to direct and mobilize their mission. They live within the certain expectation that he is always prepared to act dynamically in and through them insofar as they open themselves to him.

Taking his lead from a modern theologian whose tradition is radically different from Pentecostalism, but whose doctrine of the Spirit is equally as high, H. J. Schultz points out the immediacy and relevancy of the mood of expectancy that the times require of all Christians:

> Teilhard de Chardin tended to regard pessimism as a more insidious poison than atheism. Eager expectancy is *the* realm of meeting with a God who still has plans for the world and

who seeks fellow workers in creating the new universe, the "new *oikumene*". Because we believe that God exists neither in nor above the world but rather *for* it and *with* it, our relationship to him must primarily be one of being his companions, suffering with him and sharing him with others. The will to keep in step with God, to be in harmony with God, to agree to what he expects us to do and to accept what he does not want us to do, to accept what is ours and what remains unique to him: that is faith. It is a way of life rather than a dogmatic system.

The piety of our time is no longer to be vertical but horizontal in its emphasis. It is an adventure, a risk, an experiment. It has many surprises in store for us but it will also bring with it new certainties, new attitudes with which we shall find it quite possible to live.[1]

Although Schultz does not mention the Spirit by name, his references to "eager expectancy," "meeting with a God who . . . has plans," "the will to keep in step with God, to be in harmony with God, to agree to what he expects," is nothing other than a description of the interaction of God's personal enabling power with man's responsiveness.

Jesus communicated three truths about the power needed to make the mission of God fully operative: (1) The source of the enabling power to obey in love is the Spirit of Christ himself. (2) This power is freely available to all men who seek to live in conformity with the truth. (3) An attitude of anticipation is essential to recognizing the complete, pervasive operation of the Spirit. Perhaps these three abstract ideas can be illustrated in the contemporary context by the account of what happened to a western missionary in an Asian capital city, where he was living temporarily several years ago.

The pastor was sitting at his desk opening the mail one morning when the telephone rang. On the other end of the wire was an Asian voice speaking excellent English. The owner of the voice identified himself as a professor of English literature at one of the universities located in the city. He went on to explain that his area of special interest was the literature of sixteenth-century England, and that this had brought him into contact with the Book of Common Prayer and the writings of various Anglican divines of the period. He said that he had developed a number of questions about what he had been reading, especially about the theological premises underlying the literary forms. He wanted to talk them out with an Anglican priest, he continued, which is why he called.

The clergyman tried to put the professor off, offering to refer him to several local clergy, some of whom were good scholars, all of whom would be able to discuss these things more adequately in the language of the country. Undeterred, the teacher reminded the preacher that his field was *English* literature and that he would prefer to speak about it in the language in which it was written. Finally, the missionary agreed to meet the professor the same week, and that first encounter led into a series of sessions which extended over a period of many months.

It became quickly obvious to the minister that the teacher's questions were not only about sixteenth-century literature. Whether he realized it at first or not, the professor was using his professional inquisitiveness as a springboard from which to dive into the depths of Christian theology and measure them against the profundities of his own Buddhist beliefs. To the professor it soon became apparent that the pastor was not particularly adept in interpreting the minds of Elizabethan theologians. Nor, strangely, did he seem particularly concerned with convincing him of the correctness of the Christian position. He appeared primarily interested in exploring with the professor both the differences and the points of contact between Buddhism and Christianity.

Over the months the conversations began to have a deep impact on both men. Each was stirred and changed in his own way by the honest and sometimes critical dialogue. The adjustment in the professor's life was more overtly dramatic. Eventually, after continuing the exchange with another priest, he asked to be baptized. He chose to become a member of an international congregation in that Asian capital. There he has quite naturally assumed the role of bridge person, interpreting his own civilization to western Christians, and explaining the Christian underpinnings of western culture—now from an interior perspective—to his own students. Moreover, he bears within his own life the interplay of Buddhism and Christianity, having found an accommodation, perhaps even a meeting, with which he can live creatively.

For his part, the priest testifies that he came away from the experience a different person inside. By facing the searching questions, the articulate judgments, and the warm humanity of the professor, his own faith was sharpened even as his appreciation of an eastern religion was deepened. Looking back on the event, he believes that the Spirit of Jesus Christ himself entered the door the first time the professor walked into his study, and that his enlightening presence was evident throughout the conversations.

The initiating and enabling power of the Spirit burns steadily through this account of the professor and the priest, two pilgrims who walked along a questing road together for a while. When the opportunity for an encounter in mission presented itself to the pastor, his immediate response was to dismiss this call to enter into a new and unknown situation and to dispose of his responsibility by shifting it to others. But the Spirit persisted. He persisted through the person of a Buddhist scholar who had urgent business of a personal and professional nature to pursue, the business of seeking the truth. The urgency was provided by the Spirit, who had prepared the professor for a deeper confrontation with himself through the unlikely medium of English literature, itself the product of Spirit-filled men who had artfully put their convictions on paper four hundred years before. And through it all, the Spirit of truth taught both men, more fully than they realized at the time, to keep their lives open in expectancy for his coming again in the most unpredictable and improbable of situations.

When the disciples assembled in Jerusalem on the day of Pentecost, they were "all with one accord in one place" (Acts 2:1, KJV). The God who wills wholeness continues to call Christians to be "with one accord in one place." In the present age the "one place" is none other than this single planet of interdependent people. The "one accord" into which we are being drawn is none other than that unity of purpose which can make a wonderfully diverse—though tragically divided—church a unique instrument of God's will. Unity of structure and doctrine may still be elusive, but unity of purpose need not be, if it is based on that essential attitude of corporate anticipation and openness which constantly awaits the fresh coming of Christ's Spirit to stir us, to teach us, to elicit love in us, to move us outward and onward—each in his own way—to share that love with other men.

PART TWO

THE RESPONSE

VI

YESTERDAY, TODAY, AND TOMORROW

God calls men to be partners with him in his continuous mission of creating and perfecting the world. Each person who answers the summons is sent forth and set free to fashion his own response in concrete circumstances, in particular places, at specific times. The same exactitude present in dispatching Moses to confront a particular Pharaoh in Egypt or in directing Saul to meet a certain man on a specific street in Damascus is also involved in the compacts God makes with other men. Precisely because God's mission impinges upon real persons and authentic situations, it may be expected to arouse antipathy as well as receptivity, for this world is thoroughly penetrated with private and personal interests which contradict his will to wholeness. Facing the prospect of mixed reactions to their efforts, God's partners strive to present the gospel with clarity and pertinence. Clarity comes by coupling whatever words are uttered to concrete actions which meet human need. Pertinence is rooted in the ability to approach every person, every group, every circumstance as unique. Giving life to the entire process is the motivating and illuminating power of God's Spirit, who nurtures in responsive men that expectancy and adaptability which is essential to creativity in the midst of constant change.

As even a swift survey of history will reveal, the responses of Christians to the call to go and serve have varied remarkably, depending on time, place, need, and inspiration. Over the centuries a vast array of *modes* have been adopted to approach others with the gospel, to prompt conversions to Christ, to facilitate the growth of the church. To put these methods into play, an equally wide assortment of *means* have been employed. In contemplating how God's mission is meant to proceed in the years ahead, it would be well to consider carefully where it has already gone, using these two broad categories of *modes* and *means* as convenient sorting boxes. Only a very few of the types of response concocted by human ingenuity in concert with the Spirit can be cited and examined. But some general conclusions may be drawn about past performance, and certain criteria established for future action.

A word of caution is necessary at the outset, however. When scanning history so superficially, we would be wise to avoid hasty or wholesale judgments on techniques or agencies developed in the past. Some responses to God's call to mission were spectacularly successful by one standard or another. Some were obviously ill-advised from various viewpoints. Some may seem strange, even repugnant, to modern men. Whether they succeeded or failed, either in purely human terms or in divine perspective, the important thing to remember is that these earlier responses may have been highly desirable, entirely appropriate, or perhaps merely inevitable in their day. But while easy condemnation is pointless, slavish imitation is equally inadequate, for it is doubtful that any past manner or instrument is exactly suited to the present age.

Despite the potential injustice of forcing men and movements into analytical straitjackets, the following general *modes* of mission have been fashioned across the span of history by Spirited Christians themselves. A surprising number of individuals, groups, incidents and movements seem to slip into them quite comfortably.[1]

The influence of rulers. Beginning with the third-century baptism of King Tiridates of Armenia and extending down to the twentieth-century conversion of African tribal chiefs, such as Khama Baikano of Bechuanaland (Lesotho), Christians have used persuasion at the top of the political or social order as a way of almost automatically reaping converts at the lower levels. While the dangers of instant Christianity by decree are obvious, the wisdom of bringing whole peoples to the gospel, rather than isolated individuals, can be strongly argued.[2]

The inducement of civil power. Whether it was Teutonic Knights conquering pagan Prussians for God and gain in the thirteenth century, missionaries to China having their freedom to evangelize guaranteed by gunboats in the nineteenth, or Portuguese priests serving as functionaries of the state in Angola and Mozambique in the twentieth, the church has often relied on the power of the state, in overt or subtle forms, to aid the evangelistic cause.[3]

The appeal to local customs. A wide variety of approaches have been made by Christians through the religious and cultural beliefs already held by other men. In the eighth century, for example, Boniface felled the sacred German oak of Thor at Geismar to demonstrate the superiority of the Christian faith. When he remained unharmed people acknowledged the supremacy of the God he proclaimed. Nine hundred years later, on the other hand, Roberto de Nobili, the Jesuit missionary to India, incorporated Indian language, dress, customs, and prejudices into his own exposition of the Good News in order to illustrate its universality.[4]

The appeal to intellectual and aesthetic elements. Ramón Lull (1235-1315), one of the most scholarly, creative, and courageous missionaries in history, addressed himself to the minds of the Saracens. In developing the first carefully thought-out rationale for mission, he learned the language of these Moslems thoroughly, composed a book in which the Christian truth would be demonstrated to them by reason, and personally carried his well-conceived argument into their very midst. At the turn of the twentieth century, the Brahman-born convert Naravan Vaman Tilak sought to open Indian minds to Christ through poetry. Up until his time no Indian Christian had made so great a contribution to the presentation of the gospel in a literary form.[5]

The use of special secular skills. Matteo Ricci, the most famous Roman Catholic missionary to the East aside from Francis Xavier, gained the confidence of the sixteenth-century imperial court in China through his ability to fix clocks and make maps. His successor, Johann Adam Schall von Bell, further impressed the Chinese with his competence in astronomy, and was eventually made a member of the board which regulated the imperial calendar. Certain mission societies at the dawn of the nineteenth century were convinced that civilization had to precede evangelization. As a consequence, the earliest missionaries sent to the cannibalistic islands of the South Pacific were mainly artisans skilled in various trades but theologically untutored.[6]

The establishment of isolated model communities. In seventeenth-century Paraguay, the Jesuits gathered large numbers of simple people into huge villages called "reductions" to insure protection, economic stability, education, and Christianization. But because these communities inhibited the development of initiative in their residents, they disappeared within a hundred years. Three centuries later, in Africa, Roman Catholics created a similar system of Christian enclaves, this time for freed slaves, especially children. A middle way between total separation from and complete absorption of the surrounding culture was developed by a Flemish Jesuit in the late nineteenth century. The unique feature of this *ferme-chappele* idea was the establishment of Christian communities adjacent to non-Christian villages to permit interaction without intimidation.[7]

Buying converts. The purchase of converts was a common practice in Russia in the eighteenth century. The vigorous Metropolitan of Kazan, Luke Konashevich, actually went so far as to set up a business-like enterprise to dispense favors and rewards to newly bought Christians. While this approach quickly evangelized whole areas of the country, subsequent defections to Islam demonstrated its inherent weakness.[8]

Determined cooperation. Using considerable vision and imagination, the British Church Missionary Society sent teams of missionaries to help ancient indigenous churches strengthen their own life and witness without compromising their integrity: to the Syrian Christians of South India in 1816, and to the Coptic Churches of Egypt and Ethiopia two years later. An altogether different variation of ecumenical action was demonstrated in the last century by the now-lapsed British-Prussian venture which established a joint bishopric in Jerusalem. The bishop, who was always to be an Anglican, was appointed alternately by the crowns of England and Prussia. More overtly evangelistic than the other two approaches to cooperation, the interdenominational China Inland Mission, founded by Hudson Taylor in 1865, prospered so well that it became for a time the largest mission in the world.[9]

The comprehensive pattern. The nineteenth century has been called the great missionary century. For purposes of analysis historians actually mark its limits from the start of the French Revolution in 1789 to the beginning of the First World War in 1914. One of the most remarkable accomplishments of this period was the creation of an overall approach to evangelism in a highly organized and technically competent way. Such a comprehensive pattern involved various efforts in education, medicine, agriculture, publishing, and industrial development, as well as in communicating the substance of the gospel. Sometimes a single mission would utilize all of these elements. More often, only one or two would be attempted in any particular place. However, in this period it was generally accepted for the first time that a total approach to man's condition was the best way to demonstrate the all-embracing love of Christ.[10]

As the methods chosen by Christians to proclaim the Good News have been manifold, so have the *means.* Here are some examples of the most typical instrumentalities used over the centuries:

Slaves, merchants, travelers, and colonists. The earliest bearers of the Christian message were itinerant missionaries, whether by force, choice, or accident. This precedent has held firm to the present time as one of the most effective—though underrated—ways of missionary action. It is likely that Christianity originally spread into central Asia through the capture and exile of believers in innumerable raids and small-scale wars, as well as through the ceaseless peregrinations of caravanning traders. Russian Orthodox missionaries first came to North America in 1794 through the insistence of a lay merchant named Shelekhov. Protestantism marched into the modern missionary movement hand-in-hand with British and Dutch commercial interests in Asia and elsewhere. Chaplains of the Dutch East India Company in Indonesia and Ceylon moved beyond pastoral care for European employees into evangelism among indigenous non-Christians. Despite a policy of noninterference in local customs, the same thing happened with the British in India. Although the Society for the Propagation of the Gospel in Foreign Parts was founded in 1701 primarily to care for English colonists in America, it also encouraged the conversion of heathens and infidels.[11]

Monastic communities. Christianity first reached China in the early part of the seventh century, having proceeded in its Nestorian version along central Asian trade routes. The form which the church took in China was mainly monastic, which commended itself to the Buddhist tradition. Unlike their simpler European counterparts, the unorthodox Nestorian monks were learned and sophisticated, and their mode of evangelism doubtless bore a literate, intellectual mark.[12]

Religious orders. Francis of Assisi's journey to Egypt in 1219 to present the Christian claim to the Sultan marked the beginning of a radical shift in missionary methods and means. The center of mission moved from the monasteries to the mendicant societies such as the

Franciscans and Dominicans. The former brought simplicity, joy, and service to the poor into the missionary enterprise. The latter contributed intellectual competence, especially through preaching. Both groups sent their members to the ends of the earth as they were recognized in each era. Later the Jesuits and other orders brought new and original gifts to the movement.[13]

Lay brotherhoods. Official hostility to foreign missionaries in Vietnam during the seventeenth century led the Jesuit Alexander de Rhodes to rely heavily for primary evangelism on a tightly disciplined association of celibate laymen. This means of mission was so successful that in thirteen years Christians grew to number 300,000, though there were only two priests in the entire country. Variations of this vehicle were developed by the Congregationalist John Williams in the Society Islands of the Pacific in the nineteenth century and the Anglican Melanesian Brotherhood in the twentieth.[14]

Explorers. As the age of discovery began in the fifteenth century, the explorers and the rulers who supported them had two major purposes: to bring the gospel to unknown people, and to contact those ancient churches which legend said already existed, in order to make alliances against Islam. The fear of Islam was never universal and eventually subsided. But the conversion of any new people encountered in explorations was consistently taken for granted throughout this period. Much later, the nineteenth-century discoverer David Livingstone added another cardinal purpose: the establishment of trade routes in Africa. When he spoke of clearing "a path for commerce and Christianity," he saw trade not as an end in itself nor as a means of conversion, but as a way of developing an African economy which would rid the continent of the oppressive exploitation of slavery.[15]

Women workers. Only in the mid-1800s did the missions, both Roman Catholic and Protestant, begin to change from an almost exclusive dependence upon men to the enlistment of unmarried women missionaries. Before long, women outnumbered men as agents of the gospel, which indicates that their importance in the Christian mission has been too often overlooked or underestimated.[16]

Indigenous efforts. The popular view of the missionary task of the church has largely been that of men bearing the message to strange lands. But Christians everywhere have also taken responsibility for evangelizing their own people to a greater or lesser extent. These internal efforts have involved inspired individuals acting alone; they have included impressive mass movements too. In the last century the solitary figure of Apolo Kivebulaya ventured forth from his base at Toro, in what is now Uganda, to win the confidence of the fierce pygmies in the jungles to the west. In 1783 a group of Korean scholars sent one Yi Seng Hun to observe the Christian life as it existed in Peking. Eventually he was baptized and he returned to Korea, where his exposition of the faith led to the organization of a fully indigenous church. Despite being cut off from the mainstream of Christianity and suffering persecution at the hands of a hostile government, this independent Korean church grew and prospered and ultimately established official contact with the Roman communion. In India some of the most spectacular means of Christian expansion have been the mass movements among the lower classes. Though these ground swells of growth have been criticized for their reliance on insufficiently trained leadership and group conversion, there is no doubt that they represent a genuine outpouring of the Spirit in a thoroughly Indian fashion.[17]

Radical centralization. After centuries of relying upon expansive Christian monarchs and zealous and competitive religious orders for missionary initiative, Rome decided in 1622 to reorganize its missions by creating the Congregation for the Propagation of the Faith. The aim was to give greater central coordination and direction to the far-flung operations of the Roman church and to develop a single, worldwide strategy of mission. Strong opposition was expressed by Spain and Portugal and by local politicians and missionaries around the globe. It took over 300 years for Rome to gain control, by which time pressure for decentralization—released by the Second Vatican Council—was beginning to be felt again.[18]

Radical independence. In contrast to the Church of Rome, Protestantism on the whole has tended to foster independent enterprise, in spite of the fact that some denominations or societies have exhibited a degree of central control that makes Roman centralization look haphazard. A classic example of Protestant independence occurred toward the end of the nineteenth century when John L. Nevius helped Korean Christians develop an attitude of complete local responsibility for their church life under the direct guidance of the Holy Spirit. The effectiveness of what came to be called "the Nevius method" was demonstrated by the rapid growth of both the Methodist and Presbyterian churches in Korea.[19] Today there is growing recognition of the need for increased coordination among all churches, and some interesting and promising experiments in cooperation are being tried. But the very nature of Christianity always leaves the way open for the inventive, eccentric pioneer to strike off in a new and independent direction in response to God's call to mission. Occasionally the rest of the church has enough imagination and conviction to follow.

As men of faith listen to the compositions of history, they may hear God's Spirit moving through creation in counterpoint. His power and purpose are often evident in the general movements of men and their cultures, but they are also channeled in a particular way through those persons who are consciously committed to him and to that community which openly acknowledges and announces his sovereignty. The independent melodies of the Spirit played through the instruments of human society and the Christian church are complementary—sometimes harmonizing, sometimes contrasting, but always affecting each other in remarkable ways. The arrangement which results is wholly perceived only by God himself, though sensitive men may catch fragments of the piece from time to time. Yet these plural melodies exist, and no comprehension of history, either general or ecclesiastical, is complete without an acknowledgment of their interrelationship.

To understand history in this contrapuntal way is to gain perspective on the shifts and fluctuations in Christian responses to God's call across the expanse of time. The nature of God's mission is essentially oriented to change: it is creative, innovative, revolutionary. Its aim is to perfect and finish the integrated wholeness of creation, which means to overturn the entrenched rebellion of the world (as organized evil) and to direct men back to their proper relationship with God. With regard to the usurpers of God's sovereignty, the contradictors of his will to wholeness, the mission is basically prophetic, iconoclastic, anti-establishment. This is why the Romans described Christians as those who have turned the world upside down. This is why the world continues to be innately hostile to the gospel. Still, one need not read very far in church history to discover wide stretches of quiescence, accommodation, and conservatism. During these periods of calm, the church has tended to accept the established order, even to ally itself with the political and social structures of the times, to achieve various kinds of gain. The emphasis seems to swing back and forth between prophetic postures and pastoral concerns, between a life powered by explosive issues and disruptive forces to a life generated by quietly burning flames of piety.

There are obvious dangers in each swing of the pendulum (which, in actuality, are neither so regular nor so even as that image suggests). In the face of the artful provocations of the world, men may permit themselves to over-respond to the prophetic element in the gospel, which leads to self-righteousness, fanaticism, factionalism, and disintegration. In other instances men may permit themselves to be so lulled by privilege, comfort, and a modicum of success within the system that their vision is impaired, their judgment rendered impotent, and their spirits made insensitive to the crying human need of the moment. But the two extremes irresistibly correct each other, assuring productive motion.

In assessing church growth in the middle ages, Stephen Neill points out that Christianity appeared to require seasons of tranquility, security, and stability in order for the gospel to take root and for churches to be firmly established.[20] This seems true of the church in all ages. When times have been peaceful enough to permit steady growth, then the church has been able to withstand considerable pressures and respond to whatever new opportunities may ensue. As those challenges which history thrusts upon the church are met, then times of consolidation, refinement, and perhaps recuperation are often found to be necessary and helpful. Eyes do not have to turn back farther than the two most recent decades to find an illustration of this process in operation. The remarkable growth of the church in the United States in the placid soil of the 1950s may have provided it with the strength and resources to deal with the slashing, winnowing problems of the 1960s.

Within the broad shifts of current from the bank of revolution to the shore of conservatism and back again, there are lesser tides and eddies which reflect the same tension. In every epoch, in each decade, in any space of time there are similar swings of emphasis. In every given place, in each congregation, perhaps in every Christian person the counter-pull between the pastoral and the prophetic exists. Somehow the Christian faith has learned to hold these two elements within itself. Somehow every church—the whole church— has to be large enough to respect, encourage, and respond to the rebel in its midst even as it supports its pastors and preservers.

The pressures of history—and the Spirit of God moving within them—are both the cause and the proof of the fact that we are already in the throes of a climactic shift of balance in the Christian vocation. At this moment the church all over the world seems to be moving rapidly out of a phase of preferred treatment, careful nurture, and steady growth into a period of diminished privilege, urgent renovation, and prophetic involvement in social and political affairs. This swing away from the established power has been hastened in the predominantly Christian West by the winds of secularism and the acceleration of social and technological change. In the non-Christian areas of the East it has been prompted by the collapse of colonialism, the eruption of nationalism, the stirrings of traditional religions, and by the same secular gales which have been generated in Western civilization but are now blowing with full force over the entire earth.

All factors point toward the need for the church to construct a new strategy and style suited to a fresh set of circumstances. In order to explore this need, however, it would be useful to establish certain criteria to enable us to determine what is a relevant response to God's call to partnership in his mission. Our biblical understanding of the mission and the lessons taught us by the history of the church suggest these five fundamental tests of pertinence:

1. Are its roots firmly planted in the soil of a particular place? Because God is one, the community which joins him in his mission is essentially one. But if that community is to validate its wholeness and to demonstrate the universal aptness of its message, then it must differ enough from place to place to be admissible by all men. The blossom of the hydrangea varies in hue, depending on the chemical composition of the earth in which it is rooted; yet it is always recognizable as a flower of that species. So the church, while retaining its universality, must reflect in the design of its life and mission the coloration of the culture in which it is set. The fact that diversity is the crux of universality is strongly echoed in the two subsidiary criteria which follow:

a. Does it speak in the local dialect? This is not simply a geographical or linguistic issue. It involves much more than

translating the Bible and the liturgy into particular patterns
of speech or requiring a foreign missionary to learn the
language of the people he serves. The need to speak in the
local idiom requires a mission to develop its theological
interpretation of the truth out of the setting in which it
lives. Indigenous images, thought-forms, myths, presuppositions, and histories will be the lungs, throat, tongue, teeth
and larynx with which the Christian community forms the
word it has to utter. It may well be that the so-called
"heresies" which the church spins off as a result of its
engagement with an age, a people, a culture, a religion are
an indication of strength and integrity rather than weakness and intransigence. For those "heresies" are nothing
more than the distorted and embarrassing pronunciations
which are part of the dreadful but courageous risk of
venturing to speak in a new language at all.

b. Does it depend on local leadership and support? Since
God's mission is universal as well as specific, it is always
beneficial to have a certain number of outsiders active
within the leadership of the church in every setting. But in
post-Christendom, in post-colonial times, the local church
must fully govern and support its own internal affairs and
direct its own particular mission.[21] In so doing it will rely
upon its own reservoirs of faith and wisdom, of men and
money, no matter how weak and insufficient they may
seem to be to those who live by other norms. It will draw
upon the experience and resources of the church elsewhere
when useful or necessary, but in every case the initiative
and direction must remain local. In demonstrating maturity
and full equality with the church everywhere (which has
little to do with material resources but a great deal to do
with initiative and imagination), the lively local church will
seek to meet the best standards of its own milieu, not the
worst (or even the best) of some other ethos.

2. Is it open to all men? One of the reasons the church grew
so phenomenally in the first 300 years of its life is that it
offered men the option of belonging to a welcoming, open
society which eliminated all barriers of geography, class, race,
education, etc. Whenever, in succeeding centuries, the church has

maintained that inclusive posture it has come close to fulfilling its vocation, for it is meant to be the limitless community in which men may glory in their differences and immediately forget them. It is meant to be the prototype of the "whole" society.

3. Does it meet authentic human need in totality? The gospel is addressed to the entire man: mind, body, and spirit. For the church to concern itself only with what have been called the "things of the spirit" is to treat a man as less than a complete and integrated person. For the church to become preoccupied with mere physical needs, on the other hand, negates the unique dimension which the Christian faith adds to purely secular responses to the human dilemma. Christians caught up in God's mission are called to minister to psychosomatic creatures, and the pertinence of their task will be found in how skillfully they combine care for the concrete conditions of life with concern for the inner reaches of the human mind and soul.

4. Does it arouse opposition? Martyrdom is not to be courted, nor is oppression to be relished, but strong resistance to the gospel must be expected and understood for what it is. There may even be positive dimensions to the hostility of the world. It is remarkable how the church through history has become inwardly strengthened and outwardly attractive when it has been under trial. In times of stress only the truly convinced choose to join the fellowship or to remain within it. By so doing they give an incomparable clarity and intensity to their witness, which in turn may be profoundly appealing to many of those still outside the Christian community. Such solidly based respect may be worth innumerable easy conversions.

5. Is it responsive to change? At its best the church embarked on mission has always been prepared to move into unknown latitudes with vigor and vision. Various ventures have begun to drift or run aground when the agents of mission have lost their orientation or their nerve, when they have considered a port of call the final destination or, more significantly, when they have been unwilling to change direction as new circumstances have arisen. A major criterion of mission, therefore, must be a readiness to heed the changing winds of the Spirit and of the human condition and set new courses accordingly.

Instructed by a particular interpretation of history and equipped with five criteria of relevance, we may now turn to the task of developing a strategy of approach and a style of movement which will communicate the gospel in a manner appropriate to the times.

VII

A STYLE FOR THE TIMES:
SECULAR, ECUMENICAL, LAY

We have noted that throughout the Christian era the church has tailored its mission to fit the ever-changing, history-formed dimensions of each given period. To consider the style and size of the mission today, we need to measure the powerful forces which are so quickly remolding our world. Three interlocking factors seem to stand out.

First of all, our period in history may be described as an age of *this* world. The popular descriptive term is *secular,* which has been so surrounded by mystique that it has become a celebrity among words. The roots of *secular* run back to the Latin word *saeculum,* meaning simply a race, an age, the world. The basic contemporary definition springing from those roots is "of or pertaining to the worldly or temporal as distinguished from the spiritual or eternal."[1] That which is secular, therefore, is caught in the confines of time, bound by the limits of the known world, restricted by what humanity has garnered into the storehouse of knowledge and by what men of this age deem to be verifiable and hence true.

The secular strain in our age can be traced back through the awakening of the physical sciences over the past several hundred years to the seeds of biblical belief. As man began to appreciate the freedom God gave him to master and control creation, as he continued to realize his potential as a questing creature, he gradually removed God from the problem-solving position he had

76

held in the past. This has either eliminated God entirely from serious consideration in the scheme of things, making him a kind of honorary chairman of the board, or relegated him to a more remote position as the unseen architect, the ethereal dynamo of existence, the armchair quarterback of life, the magistrate in the court of last resort.

Flowing from the secular temper of the times is a spirit of pragmatism which moves modern men to action rather than to reflection. In the first section of his *Anti-Memoirs,* which is also a chapter in his earlier novel *The Walnut Trees of Altenberg,* Andre Malraux writes this bit of dialogue:

> ". . . Essentially a man is what he hides. . . ." Walter shrugged his shoulders and brought his hands together like a child making a mud pie. "A miserable little pile of secrets. . . ." "A man is what he does!" my father answered sharply.[2]

The father's statement speaks not only for the convictions of Malraux, who himself combined a life of thought with a life of action, but also for the spirit of the times.

Current critics and commentators have lamented that with few exceptions this does not seem to be an age of great poets, painters, writers, sculptors, playwrights. Most artists who have captured the attention of modern men seem to be "symptom-ists," that is, descriptive in their orientation rather than imagina-tive and prophetic. Our era is much more interested in research, experimentation, technological application, and production—with a practical, useful end in view—than it is in the arts or religion. Peter Ustinov, actor, dramatist, film director, describes the shift in man's mood with wistful pessimism:

> The world used to be a place of unanswered questions, and consequently a place of poetry. Man stood under an infinity of sky, minute, naked to his enemies and to the elements, believing in the gods, or in God, who represented the colossal question mark of his existence, and asking why in words and music and dance. Soon the world will be a place of answers without questions. Already the most sophisticated computers shower us with the answers to questions so complicated that only another computer can ask them. Without questions, there is no music, no dance,

there are no words. A world without questions is the death knell of God, ultimately of Man.[3]

Though Ustinov fails to see that new sets of questions always appear to replace more primitive uncertainties, he rightly perceives that man, not God, has become the basic problem-solver. People no longer cast all their cares upon God (I Pet. 4:7). Depending on their problem, they go instead to a physician, psychiatrist, or mechanic, a research and development company, a management consultant firm, or a blue ribbon commission. In spite of Ustinov's gloom, such an approach to the enigmas of life is neither bad nor good. It is merely the way things are in a time when man has grown up to wider capabilities.

Two derivatives of the word *secular* need to be considered in understanding the nature of our age. They are *secularization* and *secularism. Secularization* is what has been taking place in Western civilization since the dawn of modern science. It characterizes the process by which man begins to see this world as the basic, if not the only, arena of importance. It has, as we have seen, a neutral connotation. *Secularism,* on the contrary, has a partisan meaning. As J. G. Davies puts it, "secularism is an ideology which involves the absolutizing of historical institutions and formulae. It represents a closed world view which functions very much like a new religion."[4] Secularization may be viewed as an outgrowth of the gospel and neither contrary to nor incompatible with it. But since the gospel stands over against all religions and quasi-religions, secularism may be seen to be basically a competitive force.

In the second place, our period in history is an age of the *whole* world. The secularization process has led men to probe the world to its outer limits. Because scientific man is no longer limited to any single nation, region, or culture, all parts of the earth have become one huge international laboratory for exploration and experimentation. Technology has shrunk our world into a "global village," has transformed our planet into "spaceship earth," largely through the capacity for rapid communication of persons, goods, and ideas. The physical unity of the world has never been more evident, though its social or political unity remains largely a dream.

When the technological compacting of the earth meets the concurrent expansion of population, old stereotypes and buffers must give way. Proximity brings with it new anxieties and conflicts, to be sure, but it also presents opportunities for more intimate knowledge and a greater sense of community. In the summer of 1968, for example, eighteen Western nations, including members of the European Common Market, began to reduce tariffs under Kennedy Round agreements. Many experts see this as a significant sign that Europe is moving toward eventual political union. Almost instant interchange in virtually every area of life, even within the competitive confines of Europe, make this step and its logical consequences inevitable.

We live in what van Leeuwen calls "a planetary world." This is a world "without centre or confines, yet for that very reason limited and finite."[5] In that description are contained all the hopes and promises of contemporary life, and all of the fears and dangers as well. A world without "confines" is a world where men are free to pursue the truth to the edges of their capacity and to the fringes of reality. Yet a world that has no "centre" is a non-hierarchical world, a pluralistic world, basically a disorganized world. There is for the moment no ruling creed, no unifying cult or ideology. And a world which is "limited and finite" is a world which finds itself in a box, despite all of its freedom to pursue the truth. For when man is the measure of all things, he ultimately comes face to face with himself; and if research and reflection have taught our race anything, it is that we are fallible and not yet fully in control. The more we know about ourselves, our world, and our universe, the more clearly we understand how trapped we are. In seeing how vast creation is—and it takes large minds to grasp it—we realize how small we are. Viewed from that perspective, our tiny planet—crowded with restless, contentious people—possesses a kind of inescapable oneness which is both frightening and hopeful. If we do not destroy this whole world, it will be because we have managed to find a way to live together creatively.

Thirdly, our span of history is increasingly becoming an age of the *people* of this whole world. Humanism, which is directly linked to the secular spirit and to the concept of a planetary world, has come into its own. The power of humanism in a nonreligious form is evident in the proletarian pressures behind the socialist revolutions which began in this century and are still working themselves out. A religious counterpart is found in the humanizing trends within religions, particularly within Christianity. This may be recognized, for example, in the strong emphasis on the human element in the nature of Jesus Christ. In one hundred years or so, a long pilgrimage in quest of the "historical" Jesus has led to an understanding of him as "the *man* for others," a concept which "turns on" a whole new generation of theologians and the minds they in turn excite and inform. Consistently enough, one of the first points of departure in the growing dialogue between Marxist philosophers and Christian theologians is their common concern for the future of *man*.

Popular humanism—the widespread devotion to human capacity, human destiny, and human solidarity—is an ever more potent force, whether in its religious or its secular form. The people of the world are no longer content to be ruled by any elite. Small nations refuse to be cowed by large nations and are developing techniques to resist. Thus, a tiny Asian nation is able to stymie the largest Western power; and a small socialist satellite in Eastern Europe is able to confound the might and determination of its dominant senior partner. Minority groups now refuse to live and work passively in societies where they have little or no voice in shaping policy and less opportunity to advance than more privileged elements.

The identification of have-not individuals, groups, and nations with others of similar status across this compacted planet is also extremely significant. Militant urban black people in the United States have adopted African styles in clothing and personal grooming, not only as a sign of racial pride and cultural heritage, but as a symbol of solidarity with men who are reaching for full freedom everywhere. This conscious identification is further demonstrated by American advocates of black power who are equally militant in opposing the involvement of the United States government in the Vietnam war.

A further manifestation of the humanization factor in modern society is the mood of anti-institutionalism which has gripped the world. Perhaps the most striking instance of resistance to the control of life by what are regarded as closed groups and vested interests is the current unrest among student communities around the world. Students on almost every continent are protesting for an effective share in the decision-making processes and governing operations of the institutions of which they are a part. These observations from Japan could be mirrored by similar comments from the world over.

> Japan as a whole has grown economically, but not all parts of society have participated in this growth. Some people say we are moving from an industrial civilization to a technological society. Science and technology have moved so fast that many

of the younger generation, trained in the new techniques are far ahead of their seniors. But society in Japan has maintained a conservative cast which rewards age, years of service, deference to authority and loyalty to the company, the institution or the system. At the same time the big companies, competing for workers, scientists and technicians in the face of a labor shortage, are offering higher and higher starting wages, giving the young an increasing economic independence, but at the same time a restlessness because they are often unable to participate at the decision making level to which they feel qualified.[6]

The antagonism is directed not so much at institutions *per se,* as at the rigid and guarded nature of institutions as they are now constituted. Hippies, anti-war demonstrators, poor people, minority groups—are all clamoring after the same things. Their methods may differ—some protest by opting out, even as others protest by passive resistance or militant confrontation—but all are expressing a desire, by negation or affirmation, for a legitimate share in running a world governed too long and inflexibly by an elite.

These, then, are some of the striking features of our time. They are not the only factors shaping contemporary society, but they are among the most significant ones. They are not necessarily unique to our age, but they have developed an interrelatedness and an intensity not seen before. They may appear at first glance to be too Western in their origins and in their orientation. But as van Leeuwen's remarkable study of the interplay of Christianity and world history points out conclusively, the forces which stem from the Enlightenment and the resulting scientific-technological revolution are now universally operative if not universally recognized. He sums it up well in this passage:

> The technological revolution is the evident and inescapable form in which the whole world is now confronted with the most recent phase of Christian history. In and through this form Christian history becomes world history. The technocratic era, though it is not the Kingdom of God, is not the kingdom of Satan either; it is a phase of history in which the Lord and Satan are both at work. A timeless Gospel and a timeless church are a will-o'-the-wisp. All mankind, whether living at the most primitive level or in the centres of modern

civilization, is faced with a process which nothing can either reverse or hold in check—a process of transformation and of the interpenetration of cultures, propelled by the sheer force and forward thrust of the technological revolution. Einstein has no advantage in the kingdom of God over primitive man in the hinterlands of New Guinea; but in the march of history the former heads the column and the latter must follow; it cannot be otherwise.[7]

This brief survey of our rapidly changing and very complex age indicates, in sum, that any style of Christian mission which seeks to be relevant to contemporary man will be related to this world, will be universal and inclusive in its scope, and will be shared by the entire community of faith. In other (more technical) words it will be secular, ecumenical, and laic. Perhaps we can get at the significance of this three-piece ensemble by looking at it first in parabolic form and then by examining each segment in detail.

One of Jesus' most effective parables, which has become a classic in the literature of mankind, reveals how the three-fold style suggested by our times has been latent in the mind of the church from the beginning, although it has not always been acted out in practice. That provocative parable is "The Good Samaritan" (Luke 10:29-37), the basic points of which are surely fixed in every Christian's memory.

Here was a man, probably a Jew, who was in desperate difficulty, in obvious need. Two functionaries of organized religion, also Jews, passed him by. A stranger—indeed a foreigner—stopped and gave more aid than the situation strictly required and at some expense and risk. Driving home the point of his story, Jesus told the inquiring lawyer and those listening in on their conversation to go and do as the Samaritan did; this is the pattern to follow if you want to usher in the good (eternal) life.

The parable is usually interpreted as a personal injunction: help other people in trouble. But it has an inescapable corporate meaning too, indicated by the way it is placed in Luke's Gospel. The encounter between the lawyer and the Lord occurs just after the seventy disciples have returned from what was probably a preliminary training exercise (Luke 10:1-24). The broad implications of the good Samaritan's actions cannot have escaped those who had just finished a period of intense, coordinated involvement in the world in Jesus' name and under his instructions.

The basic elements of the parable reveal and fix an essential style of Christian action in the world. Although the Samaritan has become a great literary figure, we really know very little about him, apart from his religio-cultural identity. Since he was not labeled by Jesus as a Samaritan priest, we are led to assume that he was a layman. Perhaps he was a commercial traveler. He seemed to know the Jerusalem-Jericho road well and to be fully familiar with the inn. He made it clear that he would be returning over the same route again, as he may have done often before.

Quick interpretations of the parable tend to focus attention on the heartlessness of the Jewish priest and Levite who passed the helpless victim by. But it gives us a somewhat different slant on the story to raise the possibility that these two men were simply nonplussed by the encounter and unprepared to act. It is well to remember that these were professionally religious men whose function in Hebrew society was strictly proscribed and limited. Their sphere of action was the temple in Jerusalem, where they were doubtless masters of their craft. But along the rough world of the highway they were at a loss. They may have been hurrying on to perform their functions in temple worship which, from their point of view, may have been much more urgent and important than giving first aid to a stranger. Had they even thought of stopping, they may not have known what to do. The whole thing was outside of their experience.

The Samaritan traveling man, however, was in his element. The road was his world, as it is, symbolically, the world of most of the people of faith in any age. God's mission will not be fulfilled by the religious professionals. There aren't enough of them. They aren't where the action is, and even when they happen to be, they seldom know how to react with effectiveness. To place more than appropriate emphasis upon the functions of the professionals is to scale down the breadth of God's activity among men and to diminish the value of those others he calls to share his mission. His agency is the whole people of God (the *laos*), not just those who perform narrowly religious tasks. This is what the lay status of the Samaritan reminds us.

The lawyer who instigated the parable, Jesus who told it, the disciples and others who heard, and both the victim and the temple officials in the story itself were all Jews. But the central figure in the story is a foreigner, a Samaritan at that. The enmity that existed between Jews and Samaritans is proverbial. While they were of the same Semitic stock and shared the same religious background, they had over the centuries developed different cultural and religious traditions and beliefs and had established separate and distinct political systems. And as sometimes happens, the similarities in religion, culture, and politics, coupled with geographical proximity, curiously heightened the differences between Jews and Samaritans so that their relationship was characterized by continuous tension, if not outright violent hostility.

Coming out of this background, the particular Samaritan we call "good" showed tremendous courage and generosity of spirit in crossing the great barriers of separation to aid a despised and despising man. That was a daring and difficult thing to do in the Palestine of Jesus' time, and its lingering intricacies are still reflected in the rigid boundaries which separate the various communities of the Middle East today. In making his dramatic leap across a firm frontier, the Samaritan reminds us that God's mission is meant to be ecumenical. As we realize that Jews and Samaritans considered each other to be both aliens and heretics, we see that the ecumenical concept cannot be understood in a narrowly ecclesiastical sense alone. As we ponder its root meaning in Greek, "the whole inhabited world," we see that the word *ecumenical* signifies more than inter-confessional or even inter-faith concerns. God's barrier-breaking mission, which is directed toward building wholeness across the face of the entire world, sets no limits in its efforts to encounter and include all "aliens" (every culture) and all "heretics" (every faith).

The encounter of the Samaritan traveler with the Jewish victim called for a direct and concrete response. In other circumstances the action required might have been more ambiguous. But the simplicity of this particular situation helps make the fundamental principle of action clear. In order for the gospel of God to be communicated, man's actual condition must first be determined—not fancied or imagined. Then it must be addressed in an appropriately pragmatic manner within the setting in which it has arisen. In a narrow sense the action of the Samaritan's response was the most religious action of all, for a powerful message concerning love and faith was transmitted through the act of giving aid. To the injured man it must have been quickly evident that an heretical stranger was more concerned for the physical well-being of his fellow man than the leaders of his own Jewish religion. And that was truly a religious insight.

In a time when the "here and now" seems to be all that is really important, the parable which Jesus told suggests that even the Christian church needs to adopt a secular style. The response of the Samaritan indicates that a secular approach to mission has three facets: (1) Its essential action occurs in the particular context in which people live. These people cannot be drawn away into another, unfamiliar setting to be acted upon in isolation from their real world. The descent into the ditch of despair and the healing and recuperative action take place along the much-traveled road of daily life. (2) It meets a need which is not only genuine but is recognized as such by the persons receiving assistance as well as by those administering it. In this way the secular style is self-authenticating: it works because people see instantly its relevance to their lives. (3) It need not be overtly "religious," as that word is traditionally understood. It not only seeks to meet man in the dimension of his spirit, as if that were some isolated entity, nor to speak to him primarily in an intellectual way. In this century of pragmatic preoccupations, it seeks to enter his life at the point of his immediate concern. Having truly engaged his life in that manner, it can begin to minister to the whole man, to the hidden portions of his being as well as to the exposed. Eventually the entire process may be reflected upon and intellectualized, as the Samaritan and the Jew may have done together when the merchant stopped by the inn to visit on his return journey to Jerusalem.

We must not press a story which was told to make a particular point too far, but there is within the parable of the good Samaritan a paradigm, a pattern for a style of mission peculiarly well-suited to our own times. A three-fold mission which is secular, ecumenical, and laic is both appropriate to the times and consistent with the mind of Christ. Let us look a bit more closely at the dynamics of this tripartite approach and see how it may be applied in actual practice.

Because this is an age when the spiritual dimension of life is not very real to men, when a sense of the transcendent has become elusive, the Christian message will have to be communicated in a secular way in order to be understood in a purely human context. This raises a crucial problem of proclamation. What do we say and how do we say it? In a chapter in *The Secular City* with the intriguing title, "To Speak in a Secular Fashion of God," Harvey

Cox puts us at our ease about the words required and yet points out the subtlety of the process.

> The New Testament writers constantly exhorted their readers not to be anxious about what to *say*. They were repeatedly assured that if they were obedient, if they did what they were supposed to be doing, the right words would be supplied them when the moment came. Speaking about God in a secular fashion requires first of all that we place ourselves at those points where the restoring, reconciling activity of God is occurring, where the proper relationship between man and man is appearing. ... We cannot know *in advance* what to say in this or that situation, what acts and words will reveal God's Word to men. Obedience and love precede the gift of tongues. The man who is doing what God intends him to do at the place He intends him to be will be supplied with the proper words. Christian evangelism, like Christian ethics, must be unreservedly contextual.[8]

If evangelism—making the gospel clear to men—"must be unreservedly contextual," that is, rooted in a specific situation or, as we saw in the parable of the good Samaritan, directly and concretely related to a recognized need, then the problem of context and structures is as pressing as that of proclamation. What are the frames of reference in which the Word may be clearly articulated and understood today? Or as Cox puts it, where are "those points where the restoring, reconciling activity of God is occurring, where the proper relationship between man and man is appearing"? Here is where a large part of the crisis in mission in our time is spawned. It is not enough merely to say that the church is saddled with structures which are archaic, redundant, and obsolete. We must say why, and then in the light of that analysis seek to change the old structures and, if necessary, erect new ones. The local congregation, for example, which in one form or another is the basic structure of organized Christianity, may be almost totally ineffective as an arena of evangelism because it attracts and services, for the most part, only those who have already responded to the gospel. At its worst it does not appeal to those outside of the community of faith because it appears to be a closed corporation. At its best it often seems to be ambivalent about its function, and in its uncertainty it serves no purpose well.

Out of sheer confusion about its function, the typical parish is sometimes tempted to duplicate actions which are already being done successfully by other groups in society. Or when it does initiate some needed service, it has a tendency either to hang on to it too long or to feel itself a failure when other segments of society pick up the idea and carry it along to effective fruition. This suggests that the church needs to be much more certain and confident about its central task, much more imaginative in organizing to fulfill it, and much more discriminating in separating its task from its structures. Greater flexibility and pertinence will be gained when constricting and repulsive structures are destroyed and new configurations are created to meet authentic needs in society for specific periods of time. This must be a continuing process. Moreover, as certain types of sea animals have discovered how to adapt themselves to live within the constructions of other creatures, the church in the coming age may also have to learn how to live and function within other people's institutions. This infiltration of other, existing structures may be the fullest expression of the secular style and the truest manifestation of what a slave's religion was always meant to be.

In either the initiation of new actions and structures or the infiltration of other programs or institutions, the church brings its own unique gift of interpretation. Because Christians speak from a perspective distinct from that of the rest of the world, they bring new dimensions into the human world view. These may help to sharpen global vision, but they may also cause hostility and division, for the gospel speaks of more than mere "nowness" and understands the limitations as well as the possibilities of man's freedom.

An outstanding example of a secular style of mission suited to our times is the shopping-center ministry being developed at Landmark Center in Alexandria, Virginia, a suburb of Washington, D. C. Since its beginning, the church has been set in the midst of the market places of the world, though in twentieth-century America the trend has been for churches to become most strongly established in residential areas. The ecumenical experiment at Landmark Center is an attempt to respond to the rapid increase in our times of urbanization, mass communication, mobility, and specialization and to extend the church's witness into one of the most characteristic economic institutions of contemporary life. In North American society the shopping center is where much of the action is. This is where many people spend a significant amount of their time. By its very nature the market place is an open structure, so it is much easier for the church to communicate within the merchandising world than within many other more tightly closed institutions.

The Landmark venture is trying to demonstrate that by building on its assets (identity, dignity, stability, unique drawing power, a non-competitive nature, tax advantages, and good credit) and by minimizing its weaknesses (lack of imagination, limited business experience, mixed motivations, confused operating procedures, ambiguous goals) the church can negotiate with developers of shopping centers from a position of strength. The disinterest of developers can be overcome if the church is prepared to pay its own way at commercial rates, which it can do if it provides services which are undeniably useful to the life of the center and to those who sell, those who buy, and those who manage. The project has begun its services with a private day school, hourly child care for shoppers, a community information service, a theater, a creative arts and crafts program, a consumer education project, and a counseling service. In this pragmatic age the relevance of this ministry will be validated by how well it succeeds as a commercial venture. The strange test of value for modern men and women seems to be their willingness to pay the cost of something which in other circumstances might be given free.[9]

If the mission in action in our times is secular in shape, it is also ecumenical in style and scope. As I have noted, *ecumenical* is an exceedingly broad word, connoting all the intercultural, inter-national, interracial, and inter-religious realities of our compacting civilization. A mission which makes sense in our day must be not only directed toward but composed of all races, cultures, classes, nations. Beyond that, the ecumenical mission means taking seriously the wholeness of life: the unity of creation, the universality of God's concern and his desire for the harmony and integration of all human existence.

As he searched for an answer to the friction and divisiveness illustrated by the Vietnam war, Martin Luther King recognized the ecumenical concept as being at the heart of a new healing attitude among men. "A genuine revolution of values," he said, "means in the final analysis that our loyalties must become ecumenical rather than sectional. Every nation must now develop an overriding loyalty to mankind as a whole in order to preserve the best in their individual societies."[10]

Other writers, including some with scientific training and scholarly credentials, have seen not only the necessity but also the inevitability of a unified world. In *War and Peace in the Global Village* Marshall McLuhan forsees "a new macrocosm or 'connubium' " based on the electric circuitry of computers and other devices which are becoming extensions of the human nervous system. "Our technologies," he writes, "or self-amputations, and the environments or habitats which they create must now become the matrix of that macrocosmic connubial bliss derided by the evolutionist."[11]

There are those who would take issue with the hopes and visions of a King and a McLuhan. In a critical review of McLuhan's global village thesis, Tom Wolfe probes this innate weakness in the ecumenical dream:

> McLuhan . . . ignores sociology almost entirely. And at his peril. Several fascinating sociological studies now indicate that the very developments he is talking about are leading not to a "global village" but to an increasing fragmentation of people into small and rigid status spheres.[12]

Wolfe's point is well taken. Wholeness in the world is not an accomplished fact. It may not even be a trend, given the contentiousness of men. Nevertheless, Christians can see in biblical literature, as well as in the human condition, both the need for wholeness and God's desire for it. McLuhan and King stand within the Christian perspective and its inescapable calling to strive for wholeness in the world.

In equipping its overall operation for the building of wholeness, an ecumenical style of mission must allow for two types of parallel or sequential action: that which dismantles and destroys the barriers of separation, and that which patiently constructs new and delicate relationships between alienated men. To put it in traditional language, the ecumenical mission must leave room for the interplay of prophetic and pastoral approaches. When the tension which keeps these two essential aspects in balance is broken, the church tends to deviate from its central task. Pulled too far in one direction or the other, it may leave a wake of purposeless debris on the prophetic fringe or erect a series of meaningless monuments to mutual support on the pastoral edge. There is place within the mission for those who are called to enunciate in no uncertain voice the unequivocal standards of wholeness. There is also need for those who are equally dedicated to the task but who are called to heal gently the wounds of separation, including the lesions of those who are hurt in the necessary processes of demolition.

The ecumenical mission is concerned not only with tactical effectiveness in the world but also with demonstrating within the body of faith itself what true wholeness means. If McLuhan's *macro*cosm of unity is elusive, perhaps the church can demonstrate in *micro*cosm the meaning of wholeness, which may be construed as a unity which grows out of mutually honored diversity. It is clear that the church will remain denominational for a while—perhaps forever, if human sin or even human difference is honestly taken into account. Yet conglomerates of Christians from a wide variety of traditions are driven to demonstrate that they are united in God's main cause, the creation of wholeness, and together they work out new forms of cooperative Christian action which charge on ahead of the deliberate pace of formal church-union schemes.

To illustrate the ecumenical aspect of the Christian mission tailored to the times, we may turn to the experience of a small new community in Korea called Jesus Abbey. Started from scratch several years ago in a remote mountainous region of the country, this intercultural community seeks to minister to psychologically and spiritually lost young people from Korea's cities—delinquents, gangsters, attempted suicides, and other anti-social persons.

The general atmosphere and program of the Abbey are not overtly designed for "rehabilitation" as such. But it is believed that by living together in community and trying to find out how the Christian faith works in practice—while carrying on the ordinary tasks of life—individuals can be returned to health, to wholeness.

The process of renewing lives builds momentum slowly. After a person becomes oriented to the community, he may stay on for a year or more, gaining a better grasp of the faith and its workings, making a positive contribution in shouldering responsibility, helping new members find their way, seeking God's will for his life. There is no time limit on how long a person may stay. Eventually, he may even become a regular member of the Abbey; but since this involves a life commitment, only one new person has thus far done so.

Some who have lived in the community go out early and become evangelists; some send others to the Abbey; some are hoping for a more systematic training for an apostolate that will take them into rural areas or back into the cities; some envision establishing similar communities in other parts of the country. All are keenly aware of the tremendous number of gangsters, disillusioned Buddhist monks, and lost young people who need communities of this sort to help them make the transition from where they are to where they need to be.

So far in my description, Jesus Abbey seems somewhat traditional. Its immediate aims are not radically different from those of other centers or institutions down through Christian history. The endeavor to help persons find an integrated personal life and a creative role in society is a familiar pattern. But this Korean community has a much more self-conscious and widely conceived vision of what creating wholeness in the world involves. Archer Torrey, the American founder of the Abbey, writes of the realities of trying to engage in a truly ecumenical mission:

> Cultural barriers seem to be almost insurmountable. If we had been merely dealing with, say, the U. S. racial barrier, I believe we could have accomplished in three months what has taken three years here. Culture is far deeper than race. The misconceptions of Americans and missionaries, which have been so firmly rooted as to amount almost to "invincible ignorance," have been one of our most difficult problems. They do not believe what they hear or even what they see, if it goes against their misconceptions. The cultural barriers between Koreans of different provinces and different ages and backgrounds is nearly as bad as between Koreans and Anglo-Saxons. These pressures have almost broken the Christians. Nearly all those who entered here thinking they were Christians have left, sadly disillusioned either about us or themselves. Those who are making the grade came here as non-Christians with fewer preconceptions. They have become Christians since joining us.[13]

Despite the difficulties of breaking out of religious and cultural straitjackets, the Abbey community sees the renewing power of the Spirit of God opening and changing lives and using the very diversity of the people involved to create ultimate wholeness. Fr. Torrey explains:

The power of the Holy Spirit is at work. There is no question
that without it the game would not be worth the candle. With
all our shortcomings, love is manifested to some degree, and
increasingly. The power to convert is present, the life-changing
work of the Holy Spirit can be observed. People have been
changed by simply coming into the community and sharing its
life, brought into focus from time to time by outside preachers
who were able to present the claims of Christ and the privilege
of receiving the Holy Spirit in a more effective way than one
of the permanent staff. The effective ministries in this respect
have been Korean-to-Korean. Foreigners have served mainly as
catalysts to bring elements together, and as more-or-less
patient draft horses to keep things rolling from day to day.
Koreans tend to be impatient with detail and with "walking
and not fainting." They are much better at "rising up with
wings as eagles." We see a real team ministry as part of our
future pattern with permanent Korean staff members doing
the more spectacular sales side of the work, and the foreigners
doing the behind-the-scenes research and production.[14]

In a beginning way and as a local instance, Jesus Abbey
demonstrates the breadth and power of a mission that is ecumeni-
cally designed and operated. If we consider "the will to wholeness"
as a variant reading of *ecumenical,* then this community, with all of
its traditional language and images, is striving in a new way to find
wholeness under God in the areas of personal integrity, social
creativity and inter-cultural understanding. As a gathering of people
committed to the God who is revealed in the person of Jesus of
Nazareth, the Abbey is creating a microcosm of that unity which the
same God wills for all mankind.

The only way in which a secular, ecumenical mission that is
suited to our age can be effectively carried out is in a lay manner.
Even as that principle is enunciated, problems are created, particularly by the limitations of the words we are required to use because
of the inflexibilities of language. The adjective *lay* has been
overworked and undernourished. Consequently, it is really too weak
to describe the breadth and richness of the style of mission
demanded by the times. The dictionary which lies closest to hand as I
am writing this typically gives *lay* a negative connotation in each of
its main definitions. This source describes *lay* as "of or pertaining to
the laity, as distinct from the clergy," that is, *not* ordained; as

"belonging to that class or religious order occupied with domestic or manual work," that is, *not* on the highest level; as "not from a particular profession," that is, inexpert or amateur.[15] Clearly the farther it has traveled from its Greek origins the more inferior the word *lay* has become.

Perhaps *lay* is the wrong form of the Greek roots (*laos* and *laikos*) to use for our time. Although the adjective *laic* has the same meaning as *lay* ("of or from the people"), it has a different sound—the refreshing ring of unfamiliarity. To use another form of the word in question, *lay* needs to be *laicized,* to be deprived of the narrow character imposed upon it by the usurping tendencies of clericalism in the church. When this is done *laic* takes on its authentic meaning. It becomes *popular* in the true sense of that word, "of or pertaining to the whole body of the people."

A mission which is laic in style will recapture the concept of a totally shared ministry within the whole people of God. For too long the ministry has been focussed on one group within the church, the ordained clergy, and on one person in the local congregation, the paid pastor. While this generally accepted model of ministry is a deviation from the pattern of the Bible and the practice of the primitive church, that in itself is not necessarily a legitimate criticism. The damning factor is that such narrow concentration of ministry is no longer suited to the kind of world that is emerging, a world in which people everywhere wish to have their rightful share in governing the significant movements and institutions of which they are a part.

What has been described by one popular publication as the "crunch in the churches"[16] refers to the incredible pressures being produced in the church in the United States by the widening gap of attitudes and convictions between many clergy and a significant share of laymen, particularly on social issues. That gap is caused in large measure by educational differences, by the varying theological positions which arise out of the educational factor, by different career perspectives, and by an elusive thing called commitment. The "crunch" is also felt in the church in less developed parts of the world, but with a reverse twist. In many instances in Asia, Africa, and Latin America, the pace of lay education is outrunning that of the clergy. Disillusionment and defection occur because increasingly sophisticated laymen regard too many of the clergy poorly educated and overly interested in personal religion to the exclusion of

Christian involvement in the social, political, and economic problems
which plague new nations. In both instances the gap between clergy
and laity must be closed. This can happen when the central task of
the church is again laicized.

The laic style of mission implies that even the ordained
professionals must be laicized, not in the sense of abandoning holy
orders but in the sense of having their role recognized (by both
clergy and laity) as one of special *function* within the body rather
than one of special *status.* The church needs people who are set
apart as celebrants of the sacraments. It needs people who are
thoroughly trained theologically and skilled as teachers and com-
municators. It needs people who can give full time to the demands
of organizational or pastoral leadership. One, some, or all of these
functions (priestly, educational, administrative, pastoral) may be
centered in a single person called a clergyman, though it can be
argued that greater health obtains when they are shared more widely
through the entire body. But the important thing is that the
emphasis must move away from the concept of laymen as helpers of
the clergy to clergy as helpers or enablers within the *laos.* And this
has more to do with achieving a certain corporate state of mind than
it does with simply reordering gradations within the Christian
community.

The major barriers to a fully laic mission, then, are these three:
(1) the focussing of the church's ministry on the paid professionals,
(2) the theological education gap between the professionals and the
rest of the *laos,* and (3) the confusion of function with status in the
Christian community.

Two persons living in vastly different circumstances illustrate one
way in which the church's mission and ministry is beginning to break
down the barriers and assume a laic shape. One is a mature physician
in a city in the Western United States. After several years of private
theological study he was ordained to the priesthood in the Episcopal
Church. He intends to remain in that order of the historic threefold
ministry while he continues to practice as a full-time radiologist. The
breadth and flexibility afforded by this dual vocation are reflected in
these comments:

> My work in radiation therapy (treating patients who have
> cancer) is stimulating and challenging, and I enjoy it very
> much. The two professions, of medicine and of the ministry,
> dovetail beautifully in my case. Some of the patients I treat

die, unfortunately, of their cancer. As they go downhill, the families while continuing to look to me as a physician, also look to me more and more as a clergyman. And often I have been asked to perform the burial office for the patient who has died. So this is very gratifying and an excellent way to bring the two professions together. Also, I continue my choir work, do pastoral counselling, preach occasionally, call on newcomers to the church, prepare for confirmation, baptize, etc. It's a lot of fun.[17]

It is also significant that this physician/priest has been appointed director of vocations for his diocese, a part-time position which gives him the responsibility for interviewing and guiding men contemplating ordination—and, hopefully, the other aspects of the total ministry. The impact of this laic minister on persons who are working out their vocations as Christians could be enormous.

Another person exemplifying the movement toward a laicized mission is a former foreign service officer of the United States who decided to exchange the life of diplomacy for the ordained ministry. Several years ago he entered theological school and, after graduating with distinction, was employed by a typical congregation as an assistant minister. Deeply disappointed with parish life because it failed to provide scope for his unique mixture of talents and experience, he soon returned to international service with the government, this time in the foreign aid program. His first two assignments with U.S.A.I.D. have taken him to capital cities in Asia and Africa. In the first city he assisted the minister of the local English-speaking church. In the second he has gathered together a small congregation which now meets regularly for worship, though it may find it difficult to continue beyond his rotation to a new assignment at the end of two years. While there is a transient and peripatetic quality to this man's ministry in terms of churchly functions, it must not be overlooked that a major part of his twin calling is to bring his theological education to bear on the continuing work he does as an economist during the week and vice versa— perhaps *especially* vice versa. He himself puts the point forcefully:

In order to be good at either . . . the office side or the church side, it is necessary to be good at both. You cannot apply yourself wholeheartedly to the one but only half-heartedly to the other. . . . The real significance of this . . . is that in order to be good at the church side, beginning with the specifically ecclesiastical functions of preaching and celebrating, it is necessary also to be good at the office side. By being good I do not mean just performing competently within one's capacities. I mean being called on to perform beyond them, or what one has supposed them to be, and responding to this call. Out of this tension, out of the humiliation and agony of confrontation with one's limitations, and out of the discovery that one is still standing after all, comes the substance of the ministry.

I hope I have made clear that I am talking about the flow of insight and power from the office side to the church side of my work, from the lay to the clerical, and not the flow in the other direction. The latter exists. Some of the skills that I acquired at seminary and in the parish have been highly useful in my government work. But these are side benefits and scarcely justify the enterprise. Further, I have been consistently impressed with how little scope there really is for dialogue within the confines of the office, for basing economic policies and programs on "Christian principles." For dialogue it is necessary to have a framework which the office itself does not provide, which can be found only outside it. And the first question to be asked about policies, I think, is not whether they are "Christian" but whether they are effective. Out of grappling with the problem of effectiveness may come some understanding of what the relevance of Christianity to the situation actually is.[18]

As a theologically trained and ordained economist, the feet of this Christian are planted squarely in both worlds—that of the church and that of secular society. In that stance he demonstrates the broad scope of what he ingeniously calls a "secular-based ministry" and what we have called the laic mission.

In one sense it is unfortunate that both of these examples have been drawn from the ranks of the ordained clergy, even though both men earn their living outside of the church. It is unfortunate, but very realistic. For the truth remains that the normal and expected way to receive a serious theological education—at least in many churches—is to prepare for ordination. One of these men read for orders privately; the other went through a formal three-year seminary course. But the goal in each instance was the ordained ministry. By the same token it seems that the only—or normal—way of having laic ministries fully validated is to submit them to the formal rite of ordination, which then sets men such as these two apart as members of the clergy. They have, under our present understanding, been moved out of the whole body into a special—if irregular—category. In order to supplement these worker-clergy, new ways need to be found to provide thorough and continual education for the whole spectrum of the laity and to dramatize and confirm their own forms of specialized ministry, without moving them over into the ranks of the clergy. This also means, of course, that a new understanding of the unique functions of the ordained ministers must be developed concurrently.

To measure the relevance of this threefold style of contemporary mission, it would be well to test it against the five standards of mission which were gleaned from our survey of the history of the church and outlined in the last chapter. According to these criteria a relevant mission will be (1) deeply rooted in the terrain of a particular place, (2) open to all men, (3) addressed to authentic human need, (4) liable to hostile opposition, and (5) responsive to change. As I have tried to demonstrate, a mission that is secular, worldly, contextual will seek to meet the human condition in specific situations in a direct manner (test 3), will certainly arouse hostility as it attempts to contravene the misery caused by human willfulness and perversity (test 4), and will be continually alert to shifting circumstances in our world (test 5). A mission that is ecumenical, that is, concerned with wholeness, will by definition be open to all (test 2) and, consequently, will stir up the animosity of those who are narrow, self-concerned, or bigoted (test 4). And a mission that is laic will quite naturally flourish in the soil in which it has been planted, taking on a distinctly local coloration that will be reflected in its idiom of communication and the fabric of its leadership (test 1). For this time, therefore, such a new shape of mission would appear to pass inspection.

PART THREE

RESPONSE IN ACTION

VIII

THE NEW CHRISTIAN

Several years ago an avant-garde newspaper was started in England under the name *New Christian*. This new publication combined two older organs, the alert and prodding Anglican magazine called *Prism* and another paper called *Search*. The proprietors of the infant fortnightly, who represent the major churches in Britain—Anglican, Roman, and Free—wanted *New Christian* to express and serve the ecumenical realities of the twentieth century. The very title was intended to manifest a unique situation in the history of the church, for a new kind of Christian is emerging in our times.

The designation "new Christian" has a double meaning, of course. It may refer to one who is new to the Christian church in terms of time, one who is baptized and grows up steadily and quietly in the faith. But it may also refer to one already standing among the company of faithful who somehow comes to a point—or perhaps to a series of points—of radical renewal and recommitment.

Sometimes the two types of new Christianhood converge in one process, so that the new Christian may be both young chronologically and fresh in outlook. This happens particularly with adult converts. Perhaps the most dramatic biblical instance of the fusion of the double meaning of "new Christian" into one reality is the conversion of Saul of Tarsus. Not everyone comes to a new orientation as spectacularly as that, but the phenomenon approximates to one degree or another the Damascus road experience. A new relationship with God occurs; a sharp theological reorientation happens; a style of life changes. One may observe this taking place among new Christians in Iran, East Africa, the Pacific, and other places where Christianity has not traditionally predominated. One may also see it happening now in the Western world, as cultures informed by Christianity are shaken and sifted by unprecedented social upheaval and change.

A sketch of this new Christian, who reflects the Pauline image, can be made by paying particular attention to his prominent characteristics. Not every new Christian is perfectly proportioned, with each feature fully balanced in relation to all others, but each part is present in some fashion. There would seem to be seven basic characteristics on which we must focus in order to achieve an adequate composite description.

First and foremost, the new Christian is coming to a fresh appreciation of the activity of God's Spirit in the world. The new Christian sees God's Spirit breaking out in new and powerful ways, the variety of which is staggering and sometimes seemingly contradictory. These movements of the Spirit are utterly specific, speaking in different ways to different people according to need or circumstance. They range from such phenomena as the Pentecostal movement in Latin America to student unrest in Europe. It is almost as if this basic element of Christian belief and perception has been completely rediscovered after years of being lost or forgotten. The recovery is so striking that this time may be described as an age of the Spirit.

New Christians are sensitive to two significant points in this age of the Spirit: (1) There are no longer any surprises about the arenas in which God chooses to disturb or enlighten or elicit solidarity with his will. (2) There are no longer any confines or boundaries to participation in God's mission, which, as we have seen, is essentially a response to the promptings of his Spirit. This means that a new Christian regards that invisible membrane which separates the church from the world as being thoroughly permeable, with action and insight outside the church being as important as life and thought within it. As a result, church-world relationships become much more open, and exchange and cooperation much more likely.

This new attitude also means that the old value judgments over the relative importance of various facets of God's mission have disappeared. The new Christian cannot be a missionary faddist or partisan, for he sees the Spirit of God breaking into every conceivable human situation, and he knows that perceptive Christians are called to be present in each of those- crisis points. He demonstrates his belief in the limitless breadth of the Spirit-spurred mission by digging in deeply in his own setting to discover what God is doing and how he can respond to and enhance that action. And the deeper he goes, the more he realizes that he must make cause with and support others in differing circumstances, so that all may better understand what God is saying in the winds of change.

Second, the new Christian is committed to the central issues of the faith and impatient with the peripheral things of church life. He fits the Pauline pattern in that he strives to isolate the essentials and then act upon them. As the apostle did in addressing the church in Corinth—"I decided to know nothing among you except Jesus Christ and him crucified" (I Cor. 2:2, RSV)—the new Christian is able to make a fundamental affirmation about priorities.

In sorting out his priorities, the new Christian finds that he is not very concerned about theological niceties or complexities. Nor is he more than casually interested in the paraphernalia and trappings of organized religion. In other words, he makes clear distinctions between primary and secondary matters in Christian thought and life. While he may go to the mat over the uniqueness of Christ's life and ministry, for example, he is not overly concerned with the specific manner of Jesus' entry into this world. Though he cannot get terribly excited over the precise combinations of words employed in the eucharist, he may become very passionate about who is able to participate in the central act of Christian worship.

Precisely what a new Christian considers to be essential may shift from place to place, from culture to culture, depending on human needs and social circumstances. But in any given situation he will be able to say with thoughtfulness and confidence, "In this place at this time these are the priorities to which I must devote my energies." He has closely observed his world, scanned the gospel for its particular relevance, and made the choices on which he feels compelled to act.

Third, the new Christian is more concerned with communication than with conversion. He wants to make the basic truth of the gospel of Christ perfectly clear and to demonstrate positively how it is related to the underlying issues of life. This is why he is impatient with peripheral things which weaken and detract from the core concern. The same clarity of purpose which drives him to scrape away the barnacles of religion also motivates him to live out the implications of the gospel in his own person and to involve himself as a Christian in specific social situations beyond the circumscribed life of the church. There is a price to be paid for such integrity, however, as those who have tried to be theologically honest before God and socially relevant before humanity have discovered to their pain.

The new Christian, then, is more concerned that the impact of the gospel be felt—through him and his fellow-servants—than he is in gathering converts to a cause. Conversions to the way of Christ will occur as they always have, when the implications of the Good News begin to dawn on those who receive it.

Fourth, the new Christian quests for more serious and thorough theological education. He is not satisfied with the level of Christian learning which is reflected in membership, inquirers', or confirmation classes. He is left thirsty by the mere sips of stimulation offered at Sunday morning discussion groups. He is driven to read more on his own, but still he yearns for larger opportunities to test his questions and insights with his peers and with theologically and educationally competent leaders. He knows that the great gaps in Christian belief and action in this sophisticated, fast-moving age can be bridged only when the entire *laos* is better grounded and more articulate than ever before. This demand may require reshaping the aims and structures of seminaries so that they meet the needs of ordinary Christians as well as those of potential professionals; it may involve a diffusion of the theological education process, so that local communities are able to provide high-quality institutes at regular intervals; or it may necessitate a whole series of varied innovations.

Fifth, the new Christian is developing a free and open attitude toward worship. He wants to break Christian liturgical life out of its narrow, self-serving confines and connect it with life as a whole. A current slogan, which appears on lapel buttons worn by some new Christians these days, exhorts the reader to "Celebrate Life!" That terse epigram is merely an abbreviation of the Pauline attitude toward worship expressed in Ephesians and Colossians: "Let the Holy Spirit fill you: speak to one another in psalms, hymns and songs; sing and make music in your hearts to the Lord; and in the name of our Lord Jesus Christ give thanks every day for everything to our God and Father " (Eph. 5:19-20; cf. Col. 3:16-20). Giving joyous, corporate thanks to God "every day for everything" means to new Christians that worship is not meant to be an escape out of life but a way of bringing all life into liturgical action. In order to accomplish this, restrictive rules and traditions need to be relaxed and more flexible forms of worship permitted.

Fresh approaches to corporate worship are beginning when new Christians gather informally, but if liturgy is supposed to be an agent of communication not only between men and God but also among men, then experiments of various kinds will need to become more widespread. The new Christian sees worship as a means to manifest the gospel to modern man, and he believes that its impact becomes stronger not more diluted, that its importance grows not shrinks, as its traditional confines are opened to the realities of a new world.

Sixth, the new Christian is gaining a fresh appreciation of community. He is not a religious loner, a person who sees faith as a transaction simply between God and the individual. Rather he believes that God also acts within communities of people and that in corporate response the gospel finds its fullest expression. He regards the Christian community of which he is a part to be a locus of the action of the Holy Spirit. He sees this Spirit-sparked community to be an agency for the clear communication of the gospel, both corporately and through the individuals who are parts of it. He finds within the community the forum for his continuing education as a Christian. This special community may be as small as a discussion group or as large as a parish, as pious as a Bible-study class or as activist as a public-issue pressure group, as establishment as an official board or as free as an *ad hoc* caucus. The chances are that the new Christian belongs to various communities of differing sizes, each one of which enables him to fulfill a part of his vocation. No matter what his particular alignments may be, it is the corporateness of action which is important to him.

Seventh, the new Christian seeks to remain anonymous, in the precise sense of "bearing no acknowledged name." For the new Christian, anonymity is not a matter of shrouding oneself in secrecy or traveling incognito. It is, rather, a way of demonstrating that labels are of little importance. Actions are what count. In a statement reminiscent of the young church in first-century Antioch (Acts 11:26), H. J. Schultz writes of new Christians in the twentieth century: "We remain anonymous, do not choose names for ourselves. They will be given us by others in the light of what we are."[1] As the pagan community first gave the Antiochian followers of "that way" the name "Christians," the modern world will describe us by our commitments and our deeds.

Reflecting on the vocation of Christian businessmen scattered throughout the nations of East Asia, John Collins indicates one way in which the anonymity becomes operative. He stresses the point that the layman performs his missionary role within the corporation he serves. His task, Collins writes, is to be an anonymous

> ... ethical leaven in the decision-making process. It is like in the parable Jesus told when he declared that the kingdom of God is like leaven that a woman hid in three measures of meal. Jesus' use of the word "hid" is instructive at this point. The layman's role is not to bellow out his Christian identity. Rather he is to quietly insert his ethical wisdom into the decision-making process so that the action decided upon reflects the highest approximate obedience to God that the situation permits. Like leaven, the ethical insight becomes assimilated into the final decision.[2]

For the new Christian, then, labels are of little significance. His primary investment is no longer made in a denomination (literally, a "name") but in the particularity of concerted Christian action. His alliances in making the gospel clear are not determined by traditional brand names; they are quite naturally constructed with those other Christians whose profiles bear the characteristics of his own. These new Christians, working together across conventional lines of distinction, comprise the most exciting ecumenical reality of our time.

IX

THE TRADITIONAL CONGREGATION
AND NEW CHRISTIAN GROUPS

Christianity is a corporate expression of commitment to the one true God. While turning to God is the result of an individual decision and personal faith, few are led to that action without the help of other persons who have already responded themselves. Those who have turned to God concurrently with others or in chain reaction find that they are inescapably bound together with all those others who have done the same. Jesus called individuals to be his disciples. But as soon as two or three were gathered, as soon as twelve or seventy were with him, they became a company, a community, a band. He began his public ministry by recruiting the solitary Andrew; when he ended it, he left behind a church.

The nature of every Christian community has been traditionally defined by three Greek words firmly rooted in the New Testament: *kerygma, diakonia, koinonia. Kerygma* is a noun derived from the verb meaning "to proclaim." It may refer either to the content of the basic Christian message or to the proclamation itself.[1] *Diakonia,* which is the Greek word for "service," refers to the Christian responsibility to live corporately and personally for others. *Koinonia* designates the special kind of communion Christians have with God and with one another in Christ.[2] Any group of Christ's disciples, therefore, will be a closely knit fellowship of people whose primary purpose is to proclaim the climactic changes effected by Jesus Christ and to demonstrate their truth and power by specific action in behalf of others. Central to the Christian life though they may be, these biblical concepts are descriptive rather than functional. It is impossible to treat these underlying aims as if they were programs, though many have tried.

In his stimulating and suggestive book, *The Grass Roots Church*, Stephen C. Rose does move beyond the descriptive to the functional, developing "three alternative concepts to describe the functions of a renewed church. They are *chaplaincy, teaching* and *abandonment."* Chaplaincy utilizes the priestly, liturgical, and pastoral ministries of the church to proclaim "the biblical insight into the human situation." Teaching is "the integration of this biblical insight into the realities of the contemporary world." Abandonment is "the self-giving of the church to the world."[3] This is perhaps as good and logical an arrangement of the church's functions as any, although Rose seems to see his three operations as direct and perhaps only temporary substitutes for the New Testament concepts mentioned earlier.

John V. Taylor, in a brief, three-part study called "Breaking Down the Parish," uses different terms to describe Rose's three basic functions and adds a fourth. He sees the essential aspects of Christian life and witness as being *reflection, service, worship,* and *evangelism.* While his understanding of service and worship is rather traditional, Taylor's interesting concept of *reflection* goes beyond merely teaching or imparting the facts of the Christian faith. He believes that

> Christians ought everywhere to be reflecting together on the meaning of what is happening in the world around them, confident that they will be guided by the Holy Spirit to see what God is doing in their situation, and to understand their calling and responsibility as his people in the world.[4]

The inclusion of *evangelism* in Canon Taylor's list raises again the issue of confusing the purposes of the church with its functional programs. Is evangelism a function which parallels worship, reflection, and service? It would seem, rather, to be *the* underlying goal of the entire Christian enterprise. Taylor himself seems to support this point further along in his analysis. Describing evangelism as "drawing the stranger into the life of the small, local unit of Christian Presence," he expands his theme by indicating how reflection, service, and worship are all points in which the gospel may be made clear to the uncommitted:

If the small local units are the true growing edge of the Church they must never be "for Christians only." They are the points of dialogue with the world. They are the places in which we should expect to find the unbeliever entering into the argument over a bible passage, the communist comrade sharing the battle for decent low-rent housing, the Hindu or Muslim friend joining in the prayer or even partaking, if only he will, of the Loaf and the Cup.[5]

Quite clearly, in each one of those instances of interaction between the non-Christian and the Christian community, evangelism is occurring, not as a separate function, but as the object of the entire exercise. The relationship of evangelism to John Taylor's other aspects of corporate Christian life suggests a new understanding of the connection between the Greek-rooted descriptive aims and the functional structuring required by a mobilized modern church. It appears that the relationship between purposes and function is like the intertwining of warp and woof in a piece of fabric. Together they form a strong and integrated web, or grid.

At their simplest, the primary functions of the Christian community are the *worship* of God by his people, the *education* of his people theologically, and the *action* of his people as a creative force both in their immediate communities and beyond.

The issue of *worship* is an immense one. In an age when many seem to have lost their ability to appreciate and communicate with that power which is utterly distinct and totally beyond them or hidden deeply within them (depending on how one describes that power some call God), the church, as a unique human institution, can make an essential contribution. Yet how little care and imagination go into the structuring of worship in the local life of the church. Although he is focussing on the role of the campus minister within the counter-culture of the student world, Myron B. Bloy, Jr. is also outlining an essential part of the entire Christian task today when he insists

that chaplains must become much more concerned and imaginative about worship. By that I mean not just the dutiful continuation of the tradition, but a serious attempt to discover and celebrate the sacred in the terms of the counter culture's quest. As a matter of fact, the worship of our several traditions—and especially of the traditions which emphasize

congregational passivity, words more than actions, and reason
more than mystery—are generally an affront to the counter
culture.... The task of imagination we face is immense. It is
clear, however, that if chaplains cannot help the counter
culture to celebrate existence in the rich symbols of the
Judeo-Christian tradition—in symbols which are, I would
affirm, commensurate to the mystery and complexity of
existence even though much of their power is now problem-
atical—then we may be committing the young by default to a
symbolic resolution of their quest which is not only less
satisfying but, as history has shown, demonic.[6]

Not only alienated students but all kinds of people today are
hungering for ways to be in touch with the certainties of life beyond
their own limitations. The fantastic growth of interest in magic and
the occult—even in the sophisticated scientific societies of the
West—testify to man's need to fill the void left by a God who seems
to be dead because there is so little vitality in the way many
Christians worship him. Building around a quotation from Reuel L.
Howe's *Miracle of Dialogue,* J. G. Davies attributes this lifeless
worship to our monological style:

That which should be a creative source of life and renewal is
frequently an impediment to the Church in fulfilling its
vocation. Because its worship is monological, it is no longer in
dialogue with the world. This broken dialogue leads to death,
since, as argued above, a person only comes to being in
relation and so disruption of this relation issues in depersonal-
ization and hence in death. "As a natural consequence of
broken relationship and death of the person is the loss of God.
God is dead. He is not really, of course; but to the monological
person who, like the Pharisee, stands 'praying thus with
himself', God seems to be dead. Life is no longer rich in
possibility; now it is only a formulation wrapped up in habit and
stored in the closet of religion." Having broken off dialogue
with the world, the Church has over it the mark of death, but
not the life-giving death of the cross. Perversely the Church
actually impedes its encounter with God by its monological
worship and can only be said to be celebrating his decease. If
we spend our time within the monological attitude and
consider it to be our task to draw men into this community,

we shall only be affirming the death of God instead of living in
the power of his resurrected Son.[7]

Whatever the problems are—and monologue is one of them—
corporate, public worship needs thorough revamping and an entirely
new look if it is to speak of God to the world. In order to do this,
considerable attention will be required at the parish level—more
attention than it has received in the past, when worship was engaged
in largely out of habit and liturgical renewal was regarded as a
function reserved for specialists.

Education is the second basic function of the Christian community of whatever size. Education connotes an activity less peda-
gogical than Rose's "teaching" and more formal than Taylor's
"reflection," and yet includes them both. It is a serious, continuing,
corporate process involving more than the absorption of facts, ideas,
or a heritage. The process is specifically *theological* because it seeks
to help men understand the present world in the light of the
Christian belief about the past and continuing action of God in the
affairs of men and in the unfolding history of the universe. It is
essentially a corporate action because it involves an intense
interaction of ideas, insights, traditions, points of view out of which
a relevant and viable grasp of the faith must come.

Theological education operates in two dimensions at the same
time—within the Christian household itself and beyond it in the
midst of the world. Its internal function, which ranges from the
schooling of small children to the training of theologians and
full-time ministers, is to strengthen the perception and knowledge of
the company of faithful people. Its external function is to interpret
the Christian perspective to nonbelievers, to present clearly and
attractively "the Christian alternative." While these two aspects of
theological education are distinct, they are also fully interdependent.
The internal dimension will never be adequate unless it is informed
by the wisdom and experience of the external dimension, unless it is
refined by the questions and resistances thrown up by the world.
And the external function is based not only upon a dynamic body of
belief shaped by interaction with secular society, but also upon the
people produced in the process of education within the church.

The concept of Christian social *action* is broad, depicting the
need for Christians to be involved in the various societies—local,
national, and global—in which they have a stake by virtue of their
humanity. "Social action" is a better term than the old stand-by,

"service," which has unfortunate paternalistic, patronizing, one-way overtones, or than "abandonment," which suggests that the Christian community has no useful viewpoint at all. "Social action" suggests that Christians participate in the movements, issues, and struggles which grip mankind, bringing with them their own particular contribution even as others do. They throw in their lot with non-Christians, rather than do something to or for them. They put their shoulder to the common wheel, though the direction in which they wish to see it move may differ from the desires and designs of others. In order to change the heading, however, they have to make their weight felt. Shouting orders, making suggestions, or abandoning responsibility will accomplish very little.

Action in the social order may be accomplished by Christians both individually and corporately. Christians are, of course, already present as individuals in the midst of every social issue of our time, simply because they are part of a significant and active minority in the world. The problem is to find ways to sensitize them to view and weigh the issues from a theological perspective as they prepare to make decisions and take action, and to encourage them to feed back to the church their insights, judgments, and reflections—which illustrates the interconnection between social action and theological education. Corporately, various units of the church will find times when they can and should act as a body, bringing their conviction, experience, judgment, or influence to bear on a particular crisis. But to function in this way they must pay particular attention to gathering reliable data on which to base their deliberations, and must be sure that they have worked out internally acceptable procedures for making corporate decisions and taking corporate actions. Much of the recent turmoil in American churches has been caused by paying too little attention to this last point.

Woven or oscillating through the parallel functions of liturgical worship, theological education, and social action are the three basic aims of the Christian community: *kerygma*/proclamation, *diakonia*/ self-giving, *koinonia*/fellowship. Interlaced, they give the fabric of Christian life its strength and make its pattern evident. Education, worship, social action are designed to make the *kerygma* clear. Social action, education, worship are intended to reflect the *diakoniac* goal of a church which exists for others. Worship, social action, education are meant to be channels for creating a community of harmony, love, and wholeness. By the same token, *kerygma* (as basic content), *diakonia* (as self-giving), and *koinonia* (as fellowship) are all meant to be present in each functional aspect of the church's life of mission: worship, education, social action. The absence of any one element in any one function suggests a defective church. As it has already been pointed out, the net result of this interweaving of aims and functions is evangelization, which means nothing more than making the Evangel, the gospel, the Good News of Christ intelligible to men, so that they may exercise the option to respond to the Christian claim or not.

There is one further set of functions that cannot be overlooked, though they are of secondary importance. Together they comprise the lining and the threadwork of the basic garment of the Christian community. They are meant to be hidden and primarily supportive of the outer fabric. These functions could be subsumed under the heading of *maintenance*. When we speak of maintenance, we usually think of the care of property and the other facilities and trappings of any human institution. This kind of maintenance is important, but far less crucial than it is regarded in most churches today when so much inappropriate concern and activity are devoted to the creation, embellishment, and upkeep of property. The church is meant to engage in maintenance only to permit the adequate operation of the basic functions of worship, education, and social action. Apparently a constant struggle is required to keep the relationship in its proper order.

Some will have noticed that another kind of maintenance has been omitted in my analysis so far. It is what might be called the maintenance of persons. This subsidiary function of the church is what is traditionally called "pastoral care." Stephen Rose would place this activity in his "chaplaincy" category. But in sorting out the elements of the Christian life by the test of mission, pastoral care seems to be cast in the same kind of supporting role as property maintenance. Such an assignment is not meant to give it mechanistic or depersonalized overtones. The sensitive maintenance of persons within the body is exceedingly important, but it takes place most naturally and helpfully and less negatively and pathologically in the course of fulfilling the basic functions of the Christian calling. The church, like an army, does not exist only or even primarily to give support to the persons which comprise it. Its task is larger than that. But again like an army, the church makes wise and thorough provision for the personal care of those engaged in its underlying purpose.

For almost a thousand years the normal local expression of the corporate church has been the parish or settled congregation. Without going into historical details, we can say that it is generally agreed that the parochial pattern, which was appropriate for a stable, rural/small town civilization, is no longer ideally suited to the twentieth century. Some prognoses about the viability of this aged model are very pessimistic. Many committed and capable clergy and laymen who have given their best to traditional parish life, trying to help it change with the times, have given up in discouragement. They are convinced that only a radical break with the old pattern and the creation of entirely new forms of corporate life will bring about the reform required by our age. They believe that membership in the typical pastorally-oriented congregation has become an end in itself, rather than a means of making the gospel clear to the people of their communities. They believe that the excessive possession of real estate negates flexibility in a fast-moving age and preempts the time and money of Christians who ought to be devoting a larger share of their personal resources to the needs of the world. They believe that the almost total reliance on a paid, professional ministry has allowed Christians to escape their central calling and short-circuited the broadly diffused power of the church. They believe that the overhead created by the heavy dependence on professionals and the superabundance of property has caused parishes to become too large and impersonal. And they believe that the consequent institutionalization of the parish serves "to confirm society in its present form rather than to change it."[8]

Others are more hopeful about the parish, believing that a thoughtful restructuring within the present system is the wisest, most realistic and workable alternative. The suggestions put forward by Stephen Rose in *The Grass Roots Church* exemplify this second position. These less strident critics see at least a residual place for the traditional congregation. John Taylor, for instance, welcomes the formation of new, supplemental groups, which he calls "little congregations." But he also sees three basic functions adhering to the traditional parish:

> (a) It takes its place as a unit of Christian witness corresponding with a sociological unit of comparable size.... (b) [It is] a natural headquarters and deployment point for the clergy, particularly if they operate as a team-ministry.... (c) [It] has

an occasional but immensely important function as a "cathedral" or gathering-place for all the "little congregations" in the parish area.[9]

In addition to the revolutionaries and the reformers, there are those, of course, who advocate no changes at all in the present parish pattern. But these people appear to be blind to change in the world and deaf to God's constant call to go forth into new situations where he is not fully known.

In all likelihood we have already entered the first stages of a transitional phase in the local expression of Christian community. During the transition we shall see multiple forms existing side-by-side, complementing and perhaps even competing with each other. Traditional parishes will continue for the immediate future, though there are indications that their numbers will diminish. Some of these old-line denominational congregations will hang on to their previous patterns of operation. Others will adapt themselves to new circumstances, maybe specializing in one particular facet of the ministry and attempting to do it very well. At the same time, additional possibilities will develop such as Rose's wider ecumenical parish:

> Since today's local denominational congregation can scarcely perform the functions which the Church is called to implement, we must arrive at a totally new understanding of the local congregation, based on a total restructuring of the Church at the local level. Since virtually no single congregation can support all three ministries—chaplaincy, teaching, and abandonment—we suggest the following elements of new structure. First, local churches must band together to form cooperative ministries. Within a given cooperative ministry a single facility would be used for the ministry of chaplaincy. It would conduct services designed to offer the church member the full range of Christian worship throughout the week, from the Episcopal liturgy to the silent meetings of the Quakers. Assuming that ten present-day congregations were involved in the cooperative ministry, possibly three facilities which house congregations would be adapted for the teaching ministry of the restructured Church. They would be staffed by ministers and trained laymen who see their mission as teaching. In particular, every neighborhood would have a full-time facility for the training of adult laymen. The

remaining buildings would be sold unless they could be easily adapted to the ministries of abandonment: that is, direct service to specific unmet needs in the community. (In no case should Church ministries of abandonment repeat what the secular world is already doing. They should aim at the unmet needs.) Each neighborhood would have a full-time center for pastoral counseling.[10]

Parallel to evolutionary or revolutionary changes in traditional congregations, an entirely new approach to Christian community is coming into existence through the creation of various kinds of new Christian groups. These groups are being born because new Christians do not find in ossified parish life, or even in congregations which are gradually adapting themselves to the modern world, the kind of outlet they need for their convictions. They mistrust too much organization. They seek functional ecumenism. They are committed to radical renewal in the church. Above all they want the church to be itself, to do its own unique work in the world, free of irrelevancies and the compulsion to duplicate the good and legitimate work of secular bodies. Since very few existing congregations meet these requirements, new Christians are forming their own communities to these specifications.

In the United States many of these new groups have been lumped under the rather dramatic, collective heading, "The Underground Church." Malcolm Boyd has defined this phenomenon as "a contemporary Christian revolutionary movement ... bypassing official church structures and leadership, and concerned with Christian unity *and* radical involvement in the world."[11] No one knows how extensive this movement is, but a Jesuit priest at the University of California, who is conducting a survey of the underground, estimates that there are several hundred regular groups in the American Roman Catholic Church alone. A *New York Times* article based on the survey describes the style of these groups:

> The new underground bodies range from impromptu groups that meet once or twice in private homes and then dissolve to others that gather regularly ... for discussions and eucharistic meals. Participants regard the movement as the ecclesiastic equivalent of the "free universities."
>
> The free churches, also known as "group churches," vary widely in the form they take, but almost all include new

liturgical experimentation, a concern for social action and radical questioning of traditional church teachings.

In negative terms they constitute a reaction against the paternalistic use of authority in the church, disappointment with the leadership of the American hierarchy on issues such as race and peace, and boredom with liturgy as it is conducted in most local parishes.

No regard is paid in the groups to the distinction between clergy and laymen and none to differences between Protestants and Catholics.[12]

The same movement is apparent among Protestants, though the emphasis is placed less on liturgical renewal and more on social issues such as civil rights or the Vietnam war. Increasingly there is a commingling of Christians of many traditions in some of these underground bodies, so that they are taking on broad ecumenical characteristics as well.

New and supplemental Christian groups come in more formal and carefully structured varieties also. One of the most spectacular and instructive of these is the British-based but far-flung organization called "The Samaritans." Started in 1953 as a one-man effort to listen to and counsel suicidal persons, it has grown to ninety-two operating centers in the United Kingdom, leaving only a few gaps in complete national coverage, and extends to Rhodesia, India, Hong Kong, Australia, and New Zealand. It is connected with other local and international bodies dealing with the problem of suicide, and refuses to start branches where other groups are doing the job.

Initial contact with a potential suicide is generally made through a twenty-four-hour answering service manned by highly-trained laymen who encourage the caller to keep talking about his problems. Sometimes the call alone is sufficient to relieve the immediate pressure. In some cases, when the caller seems desperate, an emergency squad is dispatched to the place where the call originates. Often the caller is encouraged to come to a Samaritan center to talk. In all cases the emphasis is on listening and befriending. As Basil Higginson, general secretary of the movement, puts it, "Befriending means that the caller may be introduced—if he wishes—to a Samaritan who will visit him, meet him in town, go out with him and do everything an ordinary friend would do—sometimes for weeks, months, or years."[13]

Although the Samaritans rely heavily on the churches, especially in starting new branches and supplying the initial volunteers, the organization is not tied to any church group officially. Samaritans include Jews, agnostics, and atheists, as well as Christians. No member is permitted to proselytize, to attempt to convert anyone or even to talk about his faith, unless he is specifically asked for his religious views by a client. Nonetheless, Mr. Higginson is able to report "that many of the Christians among Samaritans say that they find a more meaningful Christian service, and a better Christian fellowship, in Samaritan work than in their local congregations."[14] Perhaps the attraction lies in engaging in a needed and important service out of which comes genuine fellowship and through which a message about the value of man is clearly stated. Perhaps there are other dynamics, too, as the chief Samaritan indicates:

> We have certainly shown that Christians can work under discipline together, without a clerical hierarchy. Our discipline is stricter than in almost any other Christian enterprise except perhaps the most austere Religious Orders. You may not be accepted as a Samaritan. You will never be thanked. You will have to take orders (although you will also often be left alone and trusted). Sometimes, in a real emergency, you will have to take unexplained orders: and indeed you can be suspended or dismissed at any time without explanation. Yet we find that the stricter a branch's discipline, the more volunteers it gets. Of course the training of these volunteers is all important, and both clergy and laymen have to learn important skills together.[15]

The circumstances with which we are faced today, then, are these:

(1) The traditional congregation is trying to maintain its position as the essential unit of Christian community, either by stolidly doing what it has done for years, only better, or by attempting imaginative experiments and alterations.

(2) Concurrently, new Christian groups are springing to life, bypassing the rigidities of the traditional parish and expressing the need for intimate, action-oriented fellowship. These supplemental cells, in which Christians find they can respond to their own special calling with their own particular skills, may become the normal basic unit for the expression of the Christian mission. Because of their size they permit a more personal, hence more powerful, impact in communicating the gospel and enable greater flexibility in carrying out a specific task in the quickly shifting settings of the modern

world. It is not simply that we need such groups; we already *have* them—which leads to the last observation.

(3) There is too little regular communication or mutual understanding between the settled congregations and the new groups. It may be that the church will be faced with a long period of tension and adjustment. But during that time the question that Malcolm Boyd raises can be faced and possibly answered:

> Could there be a *mutually* accepted understanding of how some people work in the underground and others in the establishment for the purpose of achieving a *mutually* accepted goal: a resurrection Church? Establishment people working with establishment people, underground people with underground people, Christ-consciousness, a mutual acceptance of moral ambiguities—and, all the time, a tremendous beginning of new individual relationships in clerical-human equality and honesty, pointing the way toward the possibility of a remade Christian community.[16]

X

THE CHURCH IN THE NATION

Over the centuries the churches have taken a variety of approaches to broad-scale organization. The Roman Catholic communion has developed a tightly centralized structure with the entire world providing the ultimate unit. The Orthodox have held to a system of national churches connected with each other by a common tradition and the loosest sort of confederation. Anglican and Protestant churches have also organized along national lines, but their international missionary activities have tended to blur the boundaries considerably. If secular political distinctions can be made in ecclesiastical affairs, the Roman system has been imperialistic in tone, the Protestant scheme has been colonialistic in nature, and the Orthodox have been the most independent and non-interventionist of all.

In the present century certain significant changes have begun to take place. The breakdown of political empires, the disappearance of overt colonialism, the concurrent epidemic spread of nationalism assisted by increasingly rapid communication, and the demand for participation in decision-making by all sorts of social groupings have led to the need for rapid adjustments in church polity. Roman Catholicism has perhaps felt the pressure more than other Christian bodies because its patterns have been so similar to secular imperialism. The trend toward collegiality in the episcopate, the creation and upgrading of national episcopal conferences, the open challenge to the authority of the pope, mirrored by similar signs of rebellion at the diocesan level, give evidence of the broad restructuring which the times demand.

The churches of Protestantism, which have had a more democratic tradition, also find themselves under stress, with their coherence and integrity being pulled in at least three directions: (1) The surge of independence movements in the world has accelerated the splitting off of ecclesiastical colonies into national or regional churches with technical, if not total, independence. (2) As communions or denominations spin off their overseas missionary units, they try to hold the quasi-independent parts together in worldwide confessional federations or families. (3) A counter-force is introduced by Protestant ecumenism, which encourages the formation of united churches—without Rome, the Orthodox, and the evangelicals—organized along national lines.

The Orthodox, who seem impervious to change from the outside, have adhered to their basic structure for a thousand years and more. Yet, though they appear to be most resistant to change, the Orthodox dispersed beyond the East are raising underlying questions about the appropriateness of their traditions and forms in their adopted countries.

In view of Orthodox constancy and Roman Catholic decentralization, and in spite of the Protestant-Anglican tendency toward world confessionalism, the principal macro-unit of church organization at present is the nation. With the exception of India, the nation is the political-geographical-cultural entity around which schemes of church union have been formed in recent decades. The United Church of Canada, the United Church of Christ and the United Methodist Church in North America, the Kyodan in Japan, the forthcoming Church of Lanka (Ceylon), and the aborted United Church of Nigeria are examples of the natural need to organize Christian churches along national lines. Though not all Christians in each country are included in these first-generation united churches, the working assumption and ultimate hope is that eventually there would be one integrated Christian body in every nation under the sun, enabling the church to speak with one voice and act with one mind in each place.

The role of the church in a nation is a precarious one, involving a fine balance between genuine identification with the life of the people and a necessary independence from chauvinistic tendencies. The delicacy of the issue is well illustrated by reactions to two specific attempts to relate the church to a particular nation. Several years ago a group of American Christians visited the Episcopal Church in Iran. In the town of Shiraz, where they spent several days, they were taken to see the Church of St. Simon the Zealot. This church building had been painstakingly planned and constructed with Persian art and architectural forms very much in mind. Local tile work was much in evidence, ancient Nestorian Christian symbols were employed, and the entire structure was topped with an attractive version of the prevalent pointed Persian dome. Here was a very self-conscious attempt to identify Christianity with local culture. In that same year, many thousands of miles away, the bishop of a large Asian city participated in a service in an American parish and was overheard to express his dismay that the flag of the United States was being carried in procession, a practice common in many American churches. The well-traveled bishop claimed that he had never seen such a thing done in any other country in the world, and he was troubled by this over-identification of the church with a particular political entity.

The visible symbols the church uses to express its solidarity with a people, and to demonstrate God's concern for his children in their specific settings, vary widely. Since symbols speak variously to different persons, diverse reactions are to be expected, and they serve to keep before us the sensitive question of how the church remains truly inside a national situation without losing its objectivity. In a section of *The Secular City* Harvey Cox analyzes the ability of the Judeo-Christian tradition to separate religion from political absolutism.[1] He calls this process "the desacralization of politics." By using an illustration from the early church he points up the sensitive stance required of Christians in their relationship with a nation or any other political entity:

> The early years of the Christian church present a particularly good example of how this desacralization of politics worked out in practice. It was accomplished not by a wholesale rejection of political authority but by a conditional acceptance. The first Christians were willing to pray for the emperor but not to burn incense on his altar. The difference between these two acts is crucial. To pray for the emperor is to grant him the right to exercise authority in a particular, restricted realm, a realm defined not by him but by the one who is praying. To refuse to put incense on his altar is to deny him

any sacral-religious authority. The early Christians thus made a telling contribution to desacralization of politics and were in this sense relentless and consistent secularizers.[2]

Although the first Christians established a clear pattern of church-state relationships for their own time, based largely on their minority status and their eschatological sensitivity, that design has not always been followed by their successors. Depending on time and circumstances, the church has composed its life and mission around a number of variations of three basic themes: quiet presence, militant protest, and ambitious engagement.

The first of these was clearly played out during the first few centuries of the church's life, as well as in other times and places, especially where Christian communities have been new and small. The keynotes of this theme are moral example and verbal witness, resulting in a personal conversion to faith in Christ. The involvement of the church as a corporate body in larger social and political issues is minimal, unless the freedom of Christians is directly endangered.

The church may engage in vigorous protest when its size or, more significantly, its stature gives it or its members sufficient moral authority to speak with effect. This means that the Christian gospel and the Christian community have gained respect and will be listened to, if not heeded. The keynotes of this second theme are a deep feeling of responsibility for the entire society, a keen sensitivity to oppression, even in its more subtle forms, a strong conviction about God's judgment and a good grasp of political realities. This theme is exceedingly difficult to master and perhaps never can be played for long before lapsing into dissonance within itself. In a helpfully critical sermon on Christian protests against the Vietnam war, Paul Ramsey provides a specific instance of how easily the prophetic voice of the church can be drowned in the excessive, imprudent flow of its own words:

> In any correct use of moral language, this has been a limited war whose conduct has been held within the test of discrimination determining the justice of acts of war. But liberal religious and academic opinion has screamed bloody "murder" or "indiscriminate" war, as if that could ever be proved by the *amount* of the destruction or by the fact that it is not possible to *separate* civilians from combatants. And they have done this so often that we now have nothing to say when our

government may have let loose a real *counter-society* strike in destroying the steel complex on March 10. We have wasted our substance in riotous moralizing. We have confused "counsel" by using words without understanding. We have used the words "immoral" and "indiscriminate" with meanings they never had in assessing the morality of war's conduct. We ourselves have indiscriminately wasted our moral resources for imposing the proper limits upon war, so that now we have not the right words to say in urging upon our fellow citizens and upon our political leaders the absolute necessity of continuing to conduct this war *against the combatancy* and not—for the sake of a quick solution—against another *society,* an entire people and their stake in the future, no matter what the costs in continuing to go to meet the forces that are coming upon us in this age of insurgency warfare.[3]

The church becomes involved in aggressive engagement when it acts as if its goal were to capture and control society. The notes of this theme differ from those of militant protest in that the church gives more thought to its internal forms and its outward prestige than it does to the social issues to which it would speak. This kind of engagement usually leads to marriage; and in that ambiguous estate the church may become so powerful a part of the establishment that it loses its perspective. In his analysis of Christianity and society today, the Marxist Roger Garaudy refers to the second thoughts many Roman Catholics are having about the ambitious interlacing of church and state. He makes his point by quoting a *peritus* at the Second Vatican Council:

> A Church which is bound up with the State—a Church which demands or accepts a privileged position in society, such as an academic monopoly—places limitations on her religious liberty and on her power of denunciation.... Thus there comes about ... the gradual absorption of the prophetic by the cultual ... and the inflation of the cultual defiles the Church by blurring what is deepest in her religious identity: the prophetic element.[4]

These three themes are not always as isolated or starkly simple as this analysis makes them seem. Sometimes two or more are intertwined in one national setting, though one may predominate. At other times one theme very quickly changes into another. It was, for example, out of the firmly established Church of England that the powerful evangelical protest against slavery arose in the late eighteenth century. It was out of the Protestant pilgrims' flight to freedom in North America that a new type of rigid and tightly closed establishment grew in the early colonial period. In a few places where Christians are found in large numbers today, their voice may be as quiet on social problems as if they were either a tiny minority or an entrenched establishment.

Even when well played, the old themes are somehow no longer appealing or even intelligible to modern ears. Everywhere the strata and structures of national life are far less simple and stable than they once seemed to be; consequently, the role of a church which is diminishing in size and power is less clearly defined or understood. In an increasingly compact world of pluralistic societies, then, what function is a minority church to have? In pondering that question all three key adjectives must be taken into account: *compact* as applied to *world*, *pluralistic* as modifying *societies*, and *minority* as related to *church*.

As Arend van Leeuwen, Harvey Cox, and many others have pointed out, the twentieth century is witnessing the final breakdown of old hierarchical, homogeneous societies. There are going to be no overarching religions or ideologies in the decades just ahead. Instead, men of every nation will be faced with many competing and conflicting options. This pluralization is part of the process of secularization, the pace and scope of which is accelerated by the ability to transport persons, products, and philosophies almost instantly across all of the traditional boundaries which have separated men, turning whole continents into mere neighborhoods and shrinking the entire world into one community.

As far as human eyes can peer into the future of an increasingly secular age, it seems apparent that the Christian church will be a smaller minority in relation to the general population. It will present one choice among many as a rationale for creative existence. Yet because the impact of Christianity on history has been so profound, the church will probably not be regarded as a *mere* minority. In fact, a strong case can be made for the continued relevance of the church, primarily as an interpreter of the meaning of the universe in a technocratic age, which itself has been catalyzed by the restless, probing implications of the Christian gospel, as they have worked themselves out through every field of human inquiry and endeavor.

But in order for a minority church to maintain its pertinence, it needs to take a fresh and more realistic look at the enigma of ecumenism, at the dilemma of denominationalism.

For the most part ecumenism is regarded as an activity that takes place between denominations or historically rooted Christian traditions. But while it is true that the main thrust of the ecumenical movement proceeds along that line at present, there is also an increasingly complicated ecumenical issue within the various communions themselves. As many Christian leaders seek to respond to God's call by involving their churches in direct social action, large numbers of their constituents are becoming alienated. Some of these church people believe that the church should not intervene directly in the social order. Some feel that they have not participated in making the serious decisions which have committed them to unusual programs. Others are disquieted because social programs have not been innovative or responsive enough. This presents an ecumenical dilemma: How can the church stay sufficiently related to fast-moving times so that it speaks effectively to those outside of it, and yet keep wholeness within the household of faith itself? As Christians face the prospect of more and varied small units operating parallel to the traditional parish, they are confronted with another ecumenical issue: How can mobile, flexible, cohesive groups be encouraged to form as cells of missionary action and Christian community without permitting the chaos which results from the lack of coordinated strategy and the breakdown of communication?

In *The Grass Roots Church* Stephen Rose suggests that the main unit of the church should be organized along metropolitan lines. This is not only a plea for decentralization but also a recognition of the trend toward local action which is being felt in the church as well as in other segments of society today. This development—so important in a time of depersonalized megastructures—may mean that the primary task of national denominations (as long as they continue) and united national churches (as they come into being) will be to facilitate the work of what turns out to be the handiest local unit. The ecumenical issue here involves placing a greater emphasis on the coordination of local action, the sharing of experience and insights gained in many places and the granting of technical assistance and material aid that cannot be secured locally. It also means putting a lesser emphasis on direct initiative from the national level, except in matters of specifically national scope.

In addition, the national church (either denominational or united) is the main way of access from the local congregation or metropolitan unit to the worldwide church. If we understand the term *ecumenical* in its widest meaning, then we acknowledge that no local church is fully healthy (whole) unless it sees its task in terms of the entire world and is willing to have its ethnocentric limitations challenged, broken open, and changed by the criticisms and experiences of the church in other cultural settings. The local church must depend on the national unit for assistance in this essential ecumenical task.

One of the most interesting developments on the contemporary ecumenical scene comes as a kind of side effect of what has been considered the basic prescription. As snags develop in structural union schemes, as the pace of ecumenism continues at a plodding rate, and as the enthusiasm of many grass roots members lags behind that of ecumenically-oriented leaders, a new kind of amorphous ecumenism is evolving. The inflation of common human problems, the shrinkage of resources with which to meet them, and a frustration with traditional ecumenical patterns have converged with a Spirit-prompted compulsion toward unity and resulted in a very effective functional approach. It is represented by the wide variety of action programs that are occurring at every level of church life, ranging from jointly operated Sunday schools in small towns to the coordination of massive programs to deal with urban crises on a nationwide basis. This new phenomenon raises the question of whether organic union necessarily rates the highest priority.

Connected with the need for an ecumenical spirit within existing communions or confessions and the stress being placed on ecumenism between the major Christian families is a larger point. If, as Schultz suggests, "Christians should be signposts to the unification of mankind,"[5] then the larger and more dramatic demonstration of human solidarity will come when traditionally separate and sometimes hostile churches and churchmen can find ways acting out (and *upon* and *within*) the essential unity they already have in Christ. This double unity, which incorporates internal diversities as well as external divisions, is not easy to achieve, as the movement toward organic reunion is painfully discovering.

The problem of separation between confessional families (or individuals parishes, for that matter) is not rooted in variety, but in competition, condescension, condemnation — to list them in descending order of narrowness. The question, as Schultz reminds us, is not which church is true, but how the churches already in existence can make the truth known to all men.[6] It may be that the present confessional arrangement can serve this basic purpose as well as one united church can, if—and it is a big *if*—they can see their traditions, theologies, liturgical variations, and life styles as complementary, as being multiple options for a civilization with multiple tastes and backgrounds. This point of view does not coincide with the "mystical union" stance (which sees the church as already united in an invisible way), for it continues to strive for an ever greater degree of visible and vocal union, but a union based primarily on mutual respect and joint participation rather than on prior structural integration and theological agreement. In other words, present denominational structures may serve the business of unified witness quite adequately. If, as interdependent action grows, a more meaningful kind of merged existence suggests itself, then that is all to the good. Marriage which comes out of a long period of friendship and the sharing of mutual interests and activities may have a better chance of being lasting and fruitful.

A pluralistic society requires a pluralistic church, whether that church be a variegated yet united body or a collection of interdependent denominations. Such a multifaceted church will understand that the claims of Christ must be presented uniquely and specifically in each situation. It will strive to demonstrate the power of those claims by translating them into militant and pertinent actions for the well-being of men. Each part of this pluralistic church will be tempered by deep humility, fully understanding that it has only a piece of the vision to go with its "piece of the action." This knowledge can keep the several segments of the church bound together in general respect and in genuine need for an interchange of ideas and experience. In a nation rent by its own peculiar tribalisms, a church which is diverse and flexible in form but profoundly united in primary loyalty, mutual respect, and practical interdependence may be able to get on with the basic Christian task without being as distracted by problems of organization as much of the ecumenical movement is today.

XI

A CHURCH FOR THE WORLD

It has become commonplace in contemporary Christianity to assert that the church exists to give its life for the sake of the world. But as with all fashions, in which popularity tends to cloud fresh insight or radical innovation, the meaning of this statement has been partially obscured. When it is glibly said that the church exists *for the world,* two meanings are hidden beneath the surface. Both contend for expression at once. In acknowledging that the church exists *for* the world, we suggest that it has a significance beyond its own life which, when imparted to society, makes a profound difference. This is a matter of depth. By placing the church's very being in direct relationship to the life of the *world*—the whole world—we testify to the universality of the gospel. This is a question of breadth. Each of these essential emphases needs to be lifted out of the obscuring mists of fashionableness and examined closely for its fundamental intent.

If we become obsessed or even preoccupied with the church's death, when we state that it lives to spend itself for the sake of the world, then we confuse its style of life with its purpose. The aim is not euthanasia or suicide but life. Life is necessary if the unique Christian contribution is to continue to be made. To be sure, living for the world in an ever-renewed and renewing way will involve dying to old, inappropriate attitudes, aspirations, and actions. Large and irrelevant segments of the Christian household may have to be dismantled and replaced. Yet, life is essential—a resurrected life, a

life which rises above its own institutional concerns and is centered
in the welfare of the world.

The kind of life which will have meaning for the world today will
exhibit a number of qualities which may be gained only through a
continual process of resurrection. Among these will be a sensitivity
to change, a clear sense of direction and a commitment to
inclusiveness.

One major church in the United States has set an official
commission to work to see how it may come to grips with its
mission in "an age of baffling perplexities and staggering change."
That commission describes the phenomenon of change as

> ... a continuing fact of life, ranging from the simplest and
> slowest kinds of physical growth to the fastest and most
> complex types of social upheaval. If the world and the persons
> who inhabit it are in a continual state of change, one either
> moves positively in response to it or resists it; no one can
> ignore change or stand still before it. All change that is
> perceived as affecting one's own life, therefore, requires a
> response. To recoil in fear may lead to death. To respond
> creatively results in renewal. We recognize that not all change
> is necessarily good. But in many changes today we believe we
> can see the hand of God. And in all efforts to make a creative
> response to change, we believe we can discern the Spirit of
> God at work.[1]

As that last sentence suggests, positive and creative responses to
change mark a Spirit-filled community. When that community seeks
to conform its responses specifically to the mind of Christ, then that
body may be identified as a *Christian* community.

The World Council of Churches uses as its official emblem a
sailing ship nestled in a choppy sea over which is inscribed the word
oikoumene (the whole world). Basically the image is a good one, for
a ship (representing the barque of Christ) has traditionally been a
symbol for the church. But, curiously, in the emblem no sails are
evident on the mast. They are apparently either stowed or furled.
This, in fact, is appropriate to the view many have of the church as
adrift in the world today. How, ask these critics, can the church
move ahead purposefully on its mission unless its sheets are hoisted
to the winds of the Spirit? Is not a deft handling of both sails and
rudder precisely the thing that is required of the church in an age of

such rapid and unprecedented change? For in the winds and currents of change there is power, power to harness and use creatively in order to move on to the ultimate destination.

To speak of an "ultimate destination" means that the church has embarked on more than an afternoon's cruise for the sheer delight of letting the wind take us where it may. There is a course to be charted, a sense of direction involved. Part of the responsibility of a church which exists for the world is to have a strong grasp of its purpose. The confusion and uncertainty which prevails among Christians today may drive some to despair, but it leads them into an exhilarating quest for new perspective based on old truth illuminated by new insights. These awakened, searching Christians seek a clear interpretation of what God's Spirit is saying to men in the forces of change that are reshaping the structures of modern society everywhere, a fresh understanding of the nature of the mission of God in a time of instability and doubt, and a new appreciation of the church's relationship to the world. Moreover, they wish to rediscover that deeper, firmer authority to which the structures and processes of transient institutional life must be moored. The church's vast and valuable inventory of Scripture and tradition needs to be sorted out carefully so that appropriate materials may be selected with which to build a new and pertinent concept of our mission. To use another nautical image, we need to discover how to use the inherited materials of the faith to construct a theological sea anchor which will enable the church to move with the currents of the age and the winds of change, keeping its mission on course without being driven on to the shoals of dogmatism or becoming swamped by the swells of relativity.

A recurring theme in these pages has been the recognition that God wills wholeness for his creation. Its corollary is that the church is given the responsibility to reflect and demonstrate this will to wholeness by the inclusiveness of its life and the reconciling style of its ministry. Together with helping men to understand and live with swirling change and to gain perspective on unfolding history, implementing the mandate to create a climate in which unity may flower is perhaps the greatest contribution the church can give to the world today. At least four components are necessary to make this task operational.

First, as has been stressed before, the church is called to take the lead in being accessible and open to all people. But beyond mere accessibility and openness, it must provide an authentic and appealing option to people of every place and circumstance by its style of life and the way it presents the gospel. Just as the early church was composed of an amazing combination of slaves, merchants, patricians, and soldiers, so the modern church must cross every barrier men erect against each other and seek to include those who are different from each other.

Second, the commitment to inclusiveness must be matched with a genuine appreciation for the richness that distinct and dissimilar persons, groups, races, cultures, nations bring into the life of the church. St. Paul's profound awareness of the diversity of the gifts of the Spirit, as expressed in I Corinthians 12, for example, involves much more than functional roles in the Christian household. It describes the very fabric of life, in which every strand contributes to the strength, texture, and beauty of a truly inclusive human community.

Third, since the inclusion and appreciation of diversity does not guarantee harmony, but rather may open the way for contention and misunderstanding, the church must work hard at helping people deal with conflict. Very often Christians attempt to submerge disagreement and hostility in the name of charity and peace. The result, of course, is a phony accord which quickly disintegrates when an issue arises that people really care about. A more honest and helpful orientation for the church to have is to take "otherness" (and the threat it poses) seriously, to identify regularly the points where discord exists and to build frequent occasions into its life when these conflicts can be examined, diagnosed, and treated.

Fourth, having made its own life a laboratory in which the dimensions of wholeness may be explored and refined, the church must share its discoveries with the rest of society. As long as the church is a visible entity in the world, whatever unity-within-diversity it evidences will make its impression on those who observe from without or are themselves drawn to participate in the Christian fellowship. And as long as those who belong to the church are involved in the secular structures of society, they have the opportunity to be agents of reconciliation and practitioners of wholeness wherever they live and work outside of the ecclesiastical environment. In both ways society may be influenced and changed, though probably never totally reformed.

In affirming that the church must die to its own exclusive

concerns and find a quality of life that has inherent value for the world, the emphasis must finally be allowed to fall on the word *world*. When we speak of the church existing for the *world*, we may be referring to the entire earth physically, to secular society in general, or to both: to the emerging secular global culture. In the heyday of missionary expansion, the primary aim seemed to center on the first meaning: to color the map of the world Christian. The theme song was "Christ for the world we sing, the world to Christ we bring."[2] The motto was "The evangelization of the world in this generation."[3] But since the end of the Second World War, the balance seems to have shifted, at least in Western Europe and North America, to an emphasis on the local situation at the expense of the more remote areas. This phenomenon has led one knowledgeable analyst of the current Christian scene to comment, "World mission in America is now, in most churchmen's view, mission to the contemporary urban industrial culture, and sending to the nations is either ignored or denied."[4] If the church is to keep its task squarely on course, however, the third meaning of *world*—both here and there, in depth and breadth—must always prevail.

The living-out of the liberating news of wholeness across the world, in every nation, is the ultimate test of the universal validity of the gospel. In order for its news to be truly good for me, it must be good for every man in every place. Otherwise it is only partly relevant, partly true. Partial liberation is not what I seek. As the story of God's revelation is clarified in various places for different people, it becomes increasingly alive and meaningful to the messenger himself. In the process of sharing experiences, translating concepts, adapting images, weighing essentials, sifting out extraneous matter, the message itself takes on a powerful simplicity and clarity it only partially contains when limited to a small segment of human civilization.

Then too, the movement of the church into every setting is a test of its completeness. The church cannot fulfill its vocation unless it has crossed every line of demarcation separating man from man— nation, culture, race. Because the church is committed to a higher loyalty than all worldly allegiances, it is one of the few human institutions which has written into its very charter the mandate to breach all divisions. That charter is validated only as the mandate of inclusiveness on the broadest scale is put into action.[5]

NOTES

Chapter 1: Introduction

[1] J. G. Davies, *Dialogue with the World*, pp. 10-11.

[2] An arresting exposition of this parallel is found in H. J. Schultz, *Conversion to the World*, pp. 54 ff.

[3] Gregory Baum, "A Roman Catholic Reaction," *The Ecumenist,* January-February, 1968, p. 125.

Chapter 2: The Nature of the Mission

[1] Harvey Cox, *The Secular City*, p. 65.

[2] Davies, *Dialogue with the World*, p. 11.

[3] Cox, *op. cit.,* pp. 76-77.

[4] *Book of Common Prayer,* p. 81.

[5] A more accurate but less compact rendering of that segment of Galatians 2:20 appears in the Jerusalem Bible version as "I live now not with my own life but with the life of Christ who lives in me."

Chapter 3: The Context of the Mission

[1] Davies, *Dialogue with the World*, pp. 21-23.

[2] C. H. Dodd, *The Johannine Epistles* (London: Hodder and Stoughton, 1946), quoted in Davies, *op. cit.,* p. 23.

[3] Cox, *The Secular City*, p. 2.

[4] William Temple, *Readings in St. John's Gospel*, p. 271.

[5] C. L. Rieu, tr., *The Acts of the Apostles by St. Luke*, pp. 27-28.

[6] Davies, *op. cit.,* p. 65.

[7] Schultz, *Conversion to the World*, p. 67.

[8] Colin Williams, *What in the World?* (New York, 1964), pp. 38-39.

Chapter 4: The Manner of the Mission

1 P. T. Forsyth, *Positive Preaching and the Modern Mind,* quoted in Douglas Webster, *In Debt to Christ* (Philadelphia: Fortress Press, 1964), p. 81.

2 Temple, *Readings in St. John's Gospel,* p. 210. The actual quotation is, "Our first thought must never be, 'What can I do for God?' The answer to that is, Nothing. The first thought must always be 'What would God do for me?' "

3 Cox, *The Secular City,* p. 264.

4 Quintus Septimus Floreus Tertullianus, *Apologeticus 39* in *The Fathers of the Church, A New Translation,* p. 99. Tertullian is here sarcastically repeating what the enemies of Christianity are saying.

5 Stephen F. Bayne, Jr., ed., *Mutual Responsibility and Interdependence in the Body of Christ with Related Background Documents,* p. 23.

6 The companion motto of this same organization, "Service Above Self," bears a considerably different spirit, which reveals a confusing but perhaps healthy ambivalence.

7 Martin Jarrett-Kerr, *The Secular Promise,* p. 180.

8 Roger Garaudy, *From Anathema to Dialogue,* p. 56.

Chapter 5: Power for the Mission

1 Schultz, *Conversion to the World,* p. 65.

Chapter 6: Yesterday, Today and Tomorrow

1 I am indebted to Stephen Neill's *Christian Missions,* the concise and shrewdly compiled sixth volume in The Pelican History of the Church (Baltimore: Penguin Books, 1964) for the examples of mission-in-action cited in this chapter. The selection of particular instances and their arrangement into categories are, of course, my own responsibility. Succeeding footnotes in this chapter refer to those pages in Bishop Neill's book where more complete details may be found.

2 Neill, *op. cit.,* pp. 53-55, 374-376.

3 *Ibid.,* pp. 109-111, 282-283, 433-434.

4 *Ibid.,* pp. 74-77, 183-187.

5 *Ibid.,* pp. 134-137, 360.

6 *Ibid.,* pp. 163-165, 188-189, 297.

7 *Ibid.,* pp. 202-204, 427-429.

8 *Ibid.,* pp. 215-217.

9 *Ibid.,* pp. 270-272, 303, 304-305, 333-336.

10 *Ibid.,* pp. 254 ff.

11 *Ibid.,* pp. 120, 219, 223-224, 226-227, 231-235.

12 *Ibid.,* pp. 95-97.

13 *Ibid.,* pp. 116-117.

14 *Ibid.,* pp. 195-197.

15 *Ibid.,* pp. 140ff., 314-316.

16 *Ibid.,* pp. 255-256.

17 *Ibid.,* pp. 386-387, 414-415, 479-481.

18 *Ibid.,* pp. 177-182.

19 *Ibid.,* pp. 343-344.

20 *Ibid.,* pp. 133-134.

21 The term "local church" does not refer merely to a parish or congregation. It is used here and in the following paragraphs to indicate the church in any specific setting, in any logical entity, in any modular unit, such as a nation, region, culture, sub-culture, metropolitan area or other self-contained locale (including a traditional parish).

Chapter 7: A Style for the Times

1 *Webster's New International Dictionary,* Second Edition (Springfield, Mass.: Merriam, 1961), p. 2263.

2 Andre Malraux, *Anti-Memoirs,* as quoted in "Andre Malraux: 'A man is what he does,' " *Book World,* October 13, 1968, p. 3.

3 Peter Ustinov, "I Propose a New Tradition," *The Center Magazine,* January 1969, p. 14.

4 Davies, *Dialogue with the World,* p. 44.

5 Arend T. van Leeuwen, *Christianity in World History,* p. 400.

6 Beverley D. Tucker, Newsletter from Sapporo, Japan, September 29, 1968.

7 van Leeuwen, *op. cit.,* pp. 408-409.

8 Cox, *The Secular City,* pp. 255-256.

9 Since this chapter was written, the Landmark project has been curtailed. While full details are not yet available, it is hoped that the apparent failure of this venture will be carefully analyzed for learnings of value to other similar experiments, such as The Church on the Mall, Plymouth Meeting Mall, Pa.

10 Martin Luther King, "Declaration of Independence from the War in Vietnam" in Michael P. Hamilton, ed., *The Vietnam War: Christian Perspectives,* pp. 128-129.

11 Marshall McLuhan, *War and Peace in the Global Village,* p. 190.

12 Tom Wolfe, "McLuhan: through electric circuitry to God," *Book World,* September 15, 1968, p. 5.

13 Archer Torrey, Correspondence with the author from Hwangji, Kangwondo, Korea, June 23, 1968.

14 *Ibid.*

15 *Webster's New Collegiate Dictionary* (Springfield, Mass.: Merriam, 1958), p. 477.

16 Dora J. Hamblin, "Crunch in the Churches," *Life,* October 4, 1968, pp. 79 ff.

17 E. Finch Parsons, Newsletter from Spokane, Washington, December, 1967.

18 Quoted from correspondence with the author, March 2, 1969.

Chapter 8: The New Christian

1 Schultz, *Conversion to the World*, p. 87.

2 John Collins, "The Service of Laymen Abroad in Economic Development," *The Churchman Overseas,* October, 1968, p. 7.

Chapter 9: The Traditional Congregation and New Christian Groups

1 Van A. Harvey, *A Handbook of Theological Terms*, pp. 138-139.

2 *Ibid.,* p. 142.

3 Stephen C. Rose, *The Grass Roots Church*, pp. 7, 168.

4 John V. Taylor, "Breaking Down the Parish 2," the *C.M.S. Newsletter,* November, 1967, p. 1. See also issues of the same publication for October and December, 1967.

5 John V. Taylor, "Breaking Down the Parish 3," the *C.M.S. Newsletter,* December, 1967, p. 2.

6 Myron B. Bloy, Jr., "Alienated Youth, Their Counter Culture, and The Chaplain," *The Church Review,* November, 1968, p. 14.

7 Davies, *Dialogue with the World*, pp. 33-34.

8 Schultz, *Conversion to the World,* p. 102.

9 Taylor, "Breaking Down the Parish 3," p. 3.

10 Rose, *op. cit.,* pp. 170-171.

11 Malcolm Boyd, "The Underground Church," *Commonweal*, April 12, 1968, p. 97. See also the book of the same title edited by Boyd (New York: Sheed and Ward, 1968).

12 Edward B. Fiske, "Catholic Underground Churches Grow," *The New York Times*, April 22, 1968, pp. 1, 33.

13 Basil Higginson, "The Samaritans," *Christian Comment,* October, 1968, p. 2.

14 *Ibid.,* p. 3.

15 *Ibid.,* p. 4.

16 Boyd, "The Underground Church," p. 100.

Chapter 10: The Church in the Nation

1 Cox, *The Secular City,* pp. 25-30.

2 *Ibid.,* p. 27.

3 R. Paul Ramsey, "Counting the Costs" in Hamilton, *The Vietnam War: Christian Perspectives,* pp. 43-44.

4 Gonzalez Ruiz, as quoted in Roger Garaudy, *From Anathema to Dialogue,* p. 68.

5 Schultz, *Conversion to the World,* p. 78.

6 *Ibid.,* p. 86.

Chapter 11: A Church for the World

1 *In Search of a Positive Response to Change,* Interim Report of the Joint Commission on Renewal of the Episcopal Church, June 1, 1969, Section III. A.

2 Samuel Wolcott, "Christ for the World We Sing," *The Hymnal* (New York: The Church Pension Fund, 1940), No. 537. Wolcott, who had been a missionary in Syria for two years, based his hymn on the slogan of the 1869 Ohio State Convention of the Y.M.C.A., "Christ for the world, and the world for Christ," which had deeply impressed him.

3 Stephen Neill points out that John R. Mott's famous "slogan was based on an exceptionable theological principle − that each generation of Christians bears responsibility for the contemporary generation of non-Christians in the world, and that it is the business of each such generation of Christians to see to it, as far as lies within its power, that the Gospel is clearly preached to every single non-Christian in the same generation. This," Neill continues, "is of universal and permanent obligation; it applies to Christian witness both within what is commonly called Christendom and beyond it. If the principle is to be rejected, the New Testament must first be rewritten" (*Christian Missions,* pp. 393 ff.). This is a useful corrective to the attitude that Mott's slogan was naive, utopian and imperialistic. The fact remains, however, that much of the positive response to those words was tinged with a deep desire for extensive programs of evangelism.

4 R. Pierce Beaver, Correspondence with the author from Chicago, February 5, 1968.

5 For an extended argument on these last points, see A. Theodore Eastman, *Christian Responsibility in One World* (New York: Seabury, 1965).

BIBLIOGRAPHY

Bayne, Stephen F., Jr., ed., *Mutual Responsibility and Interdependence in the Body of Christ with Related Background Documents,* New York: Seabury, 1963.

Boyd, Malcolm, *The Underground Church,* New York: Sheed and Ward, 1968.

Cox, Harvey, *The Secular City,* New York: Macmillan, 1965.

Cragg, Kenneth, *Christianity in World Perspective,* London: Lutterworth, 1968.

Davies, J. G., *Dialogue with the World,* London: S.C.M., 1967.

Eastman, A. Theodore, *Christian Responsibility in One World,* New York: Seabury, 1965.

Foster, John, *Requiem for a Parish,* Westminster, Maryland: Newman, 1963.

Garaudy, Roger, *From Anathema to Dialogue,* New York: Herder and Herder, 1966.

Hamilton, Michael P., ed., *The Vietnam War: Christian Perspectives,* Grand Rapids: Eerdmans, 1967.

Harvey, Van A., *A Handbook of Theological Terms,* New York: Macmillan, 1964.

Jarrett-Kerr, Martin, *The Secular Promise,* London: S.C.M., 1964.

McLuhan, Marshall, *War and Peace in the Global Village,* New York: Bantam, 1968.

Neill, Stephen, *The Pelican History of the Church: 6; A History of Christian Missions,* Baltimore: Penguin, 1964.

Porter, H. Boone, Jr., *Growth and Life in the Local Church,* New York: Seabury, 1968.

Richardson, William J., ed., *The Church as Sign,* Maryknoll, N.Y.: Maryknoll Press, 1968.

Rieu, C. L., tr., *The Acts of the Apostles by St. Luke,* Harmondsworth: Penguin, 1957.

Rose, Stephen C., *The Grass Roots Church,* New York: Holt, Rinehart and Winston, 1966.

Schneider, Peter, *Sweeter Than Honey,* London: S.C.M., 1966.

Schultz, H. J., *Conversion to the World*, New York: Scribners, 1967.

Temple, William, *Readings in St. John's Gospel,* London: Macmillan, 1950.

Tertullianus, Quintus Septimus Floreus, *Apologeticus 39* in *The Fathers of the Church, A New Translation,* New York: The Fathers of the Church, Inc., 1950.

van Leeuwen, Arend T., *Christianity in World History,* New York: Scribners, 1964.

Webster, Douglas, *In Debt to Christ,* Philadelphia: Fortress, 1964.

Wieser, Thomas, ed., *Planning for Mission,* New York: The U.S. Conference for the World Council of Churches, 1966.

Williams, Colin W., *New Directions in Theology Today: Vol. IV; The Church,* Philadelphia: Westminster, 1968.

INDEX OF NAMES AND PLACES

INDEX OF BIBLICAL REFERENCES